3⁰⁰/mۑp

Cover: On the Keighley & Worth Valley Railway BR '4' 4-6-0
No 75078 climbs away from Damems on the 15.47 Keighley-
Oxenhope on 17 June 1979.   *W. A. Sharman*

This picture: Class 55 'Deltic' Co-Co diesel electric
No 55.006 *The Fife and Forfar Yeomanry* sets
out from Goole with the 16.30 Hull-Kings Cross on
28 September 1979.   *G. S. Cutts*

Goole

D1370578

£3.95

Gresley 'V1' 2-6-2T No 67645 banks a Kings Cross express out of Durham in 1963. *M. Dunnett*

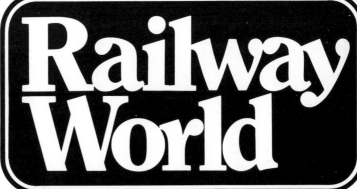

annual

Edited by
Michael Harris

LONDON

IAN ALLAN LTD

First published 1980

ISBN 0 7110 1045 5

All rights reserved. No part of this book may be
reproduced or transmitted in any form or by any
means, electronic or mechanical, including photo-
copying, recording or by any information storage
and retrieval system, without permission from the
Publisher in writing.

© Ian Allan Ltd 1980

Published by Ian Allan Ltd, Shepperton, Surrey;
and printed by Ian Allan Printing Ltd at their works
at Coombelands in Runnymede, England

Contents

This picture: Bedlay Colliery's stand-by
Barclay 0-4-0ST No 17, built 1952, drags
a rake of wagons across the weighbridge
on 10 May 1979. *C. P. Boocock*

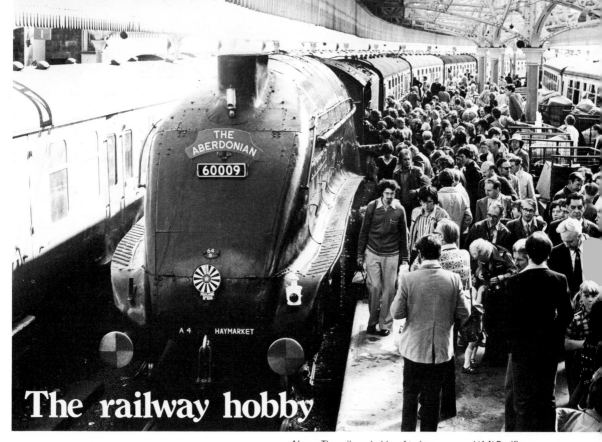

The railway hobby

MICHAEL HARRIS

Above: The railway hobby of today: preserved 'A4' Pacific
No 60009 *Union of South Africa* at Aberdeen, having arrived
with a charter train from Edinburgh on 27 August 1978.
John Titlow

These days we tend to see others as ourselves. There is the almost continuous diet of 'costume serials' on tv that are so often dramas of late twentieth century people concerned with past events and dressed up in yesterday's styles. The dialogue and attitudes don't run true. The same seems to be true of people's interests, and it is doubtful whether many of today's leisure pursuits are comparable with what our grandfathers and their parents did in their spare time. We have a high level of literacy (but this goes back 100 years at the most); paid holidays (since 1945, mostly); a five-day week (widespread only since the 1950s); 'affluent teenagers' (part of the social revolution of the 1950s); a high level of car ownership (the number of cars doubled between 1959-70). We take for granted efficient and cheap means of photography (thanks to the 35mm camera, post-late 1930s) and transistorised tape recorders (from the 1960s). All these characteristics of present-day life are recent and being so have greatly altered the way people can follow their hobbies, the extent to which they can develop them and the time that they have to enjoy them. One further dimension is that of foreign travel, and the fact that as cheap means of travelling abroad

have become available, so have the ways in which the experience can be recorded (on film or tape) for posterity. In thirty years the ordinary person has had his leisure-time and the ways of enjoying it transformed.

People have always enjoyed watching others work. Most Victorian record photographs of social life and railways — particularly — are packed with bystanders. Those days they were passive watchers, nowadays they would probably be out of the picture recording it for themselves. Perhaps this has something to do with the increase in service jobs, clerical, administrative and the like, in which all too often the work is so undemanding that leisure is taken more seriously than employment. Here, too, things have changed. Most manual jobs were so physically demanding and occupied so much of waking hours that once the daily grind was over the worker sank thankfully into pure relaxation. Now hobbies have become jobs and in attempting to face a future probably dominated by chips and micro-processors the powers that be could do worse than recognise that steam railways, say, might not be a useful tool with

3

Above: Pre-grouping railway heyday: Caledonian Railway 'Dunalastair IV' 4-4-0 No 121 at the head of a Perth-Euston express. *F. E. Mackay*

which to combat the threats of under-employment.

Before we go off too much at a tangent, it is enough to make the point that the railway hobby has reached the state it has, for all the reasons so far mentioned and also because of the enthusiasm, hard work and initiative of many people over the years.

But to go back to the beginning. We start with railways in the 1840s as the symbol of the new technology, and they were bound to attract attention, good or bad. The men staffing the railways doubtless signed on because they wanted jobs; only a few enjoyed the luxury of working for the companies because they found railways interesting. But the men who did, and who were professionals, were young. Gooch was twenty-one when he became Locomotive Superintendent of the Great Western Railway and he was not that unusual. The men involved were probably so busy making the early railways and their mechanical engineering work that they had little time to stand back and reflect.

Mechanical engineering was largely fostered by the demands of the railway system, but mechanical engineers were not regarded as yet as a profession. In October 1846, J. E. McConnell, Locomotive Superintendent, Southern Division LNWR, was responsible for the formation of the Institution of Mechanical Engineers and the first formal meeting of the new organisation was at Curzon Street station, Birmingham, where George Stephenson was elected chairman. A plaque records this significant event (Curzon St became the early offices of the Institution) and has for years adorned a deteriorating and unloved building, that, happily, is now in the process of restoration. From the professional point of view the Institution was to serve the interests of railway mechanical engineers for some 40 years; we can be sure that it provided a focus and meeting place for those more enthusiastically as well as professionally interested in their work.

In the 1850s and 1860s there was a railway press

but one overwhelmingly concerned with the industry as a commercial undertaking. Typical publications were *Herapath's Journal*, *Railway Times* (of 1837) and *Railway News*, and the original *Railway Magazine*, which dated back to 1835. Certainly there was much news being made by railways: new lines, new companies, warfare between companies, and the doings of the captains of the railway industry.

Meanwhile, railways were beginning to take an interest in their own history, seeing that the earliest events were beginning to slip towards the edge of living memory. Railway artefacts were set aside such as the presentation of the remnants of the original Stephenson's *Rocket* by Lord Carlisle's colliery agents to the Patent Office in September 1862. Then there were the fiftieth anniversary celebrations of the opening of the Stockton & Darlington in 1875. Shortly afterwards, in June 1881, Newcastle saw some carefully organised celebrations to commemorate the centenary of George Stephenson's birth. For this, apart from celebrations, the unveiling of a monument to Stephenson, draught horse processions and the like, there was also a procession of modern locomotives at Wylam station and an exhibition in Newcastle of *Locomotion No 1*, *Invicta*, *Puffing Billy*, the Hetton Colliery engine and an 1839-built example.

In short, anniversaries were occasions to commemorate what had gone before and to acknowledge that railways now had a history of their own and, of course, that their equipment was of intrinsic interest. It is pleasant to think that one hundred years ago in the height of what we like to think was the Victorian heyday (but which economists rightly point out was the Great Depression of the 1880s), men were delighting in the history of railways and of the achievements of their early makers. The Great Western Railway has long suffered from the stigma of having destroyed the broad gauge preserved locomotives, *North Star* of 1837 and *Lord of the Isles* of 1851. Both were scrapped in 1906 but W. O. Skeat writing in *Yesteryear Transport* in 1979 rightly draws attention to the fact that, during the 1880s, Sir Daniel Gooch himself when GWR Chairman had instigated the building of a shed to house those priceless relics. The abolition of the broad gauge probably presented the first major occasion for railway-minded people to reflect upon the disappearance of historical relics and of an era. There *were* broad gauge enthusiasts, amateurs and professional railwaymen and they did their best to record the passing of the 7ft gauge. Not for the first time did the railway management feel that their duty was to modernise and not to look back. Preservation appeared to involve just that.

In any case, railways were doing exciting things in late Victorian times, at home and abroad, and it was right that attention should be concentrated on current events. Railways represented the most immediate example of high technology open for study by the man in the street. The developments in equipment, locomotives and rolling stock were followed with the same sort of general enthusiasm that people display towards automobile and aerospace engineering today — the *Tomorrow's World* type of approach.

Who indeed could fail to thrill (or frown) over the West Coast/East Coast companies' rivalry in the Races to the North of 1888 and 1895? No doubt the middle class professional family man did so, but now — for the first time perhaps — there were the early railway enthusiasts as avid spectators of great events. In *The Railway Race to the North* (published by Ian Allan Ltd, 1959) O. S. Nock describes the tireless efforts of train performance recorders such as Charles Rous-Marten, Rev W. J. Scott and W. M. Acworth armed with stop-watches — and given free passes by the East Coast Route railways. Rous-Marten's articles describing the races appeared in *The Engineer* during 1895.

Railway literature, books and periodicals dealing with railway operation for the general reader were beginning to make their appearance. Frederick S. Williams' *Our Iron Roads* of 1883 was an excellent general account of railway history, construction and management. In *Express Trains English & Foreign*, published in 1889, Foxwell and Farrer surveyed the standard and performance of passenger trains, drawing some not too flattering comparisons. Railway histories were written: Grinling's *History of the Great Northern Railway* (1898) and Stretton's *History of the Midland Railway* (1901). W. M. Acworth's *The Railways of England*, first published in 1889, went through four editions before a new edition was brought out in 1899.

Earlier it was suggested that the Institution of Mechanical Engineers served the needs of railway engineers into the later Victorian years. But as the new century dawned, there was some dissatisfaction among railway engineering professionals that the Institution was unable to give adequate coverage of railway subjects and to organise meetings at which engineers from different railways (home and British-owned overseas and colonial) could exchange ideas and discuss the 'state of the art'. Local engineering societies were formed at railway works towns such as Swindon and Derby.

Then, in 1899, The Railway Club was formed — 'open to those interested professionally and otherwise in railways' — as its aim stated then and still does today. The Club was set up primarily to study the steam locomotive, but before long was, not surprisingly, immersed in operating aspects. Ten years later, this had its effect for 1909 saw a breakaway movement with those more closely interested in the steam

Above:: Railtour pioneer: the RCTS excursion from Kings Cross-Peterborough in September 1938, with Stirling Single No 1 at Potters Bar. *C. R. L. Coles*

locomotive setting up the Stephenson Locomotive Society, such as G. F. Burtt, of the London, Brighton & South Coast Railway's Brighton Works and a respected writer on locomotive design. From the beginning, this had a part-amateur, part-professional membership, as indeed it does today. But Mr Burtt and others were still not entirely satisfied and from the SLS they moved to form another locomotive engineers' organisation, this time more directly professional. This was the Institution of Locomotive Engineers set up during 1911 and incorporated in 1915. This renowned Institution served the interests of its members faithfully as a separate professional body until 1970 when it became the Railway Division of the Institution of Mechanical Engineers. The Edwardian era, then, had seen the formation of the first societies catering for an interest in railways, in which the amateur was welcomed with the professional career railwaymen.

Typical professional 'enthusiasts' of this time were perhaps summed up by Mr E. F. S. Notter, King's Cross District Locomotive Superintendent 1905-24. He was a railway enthusiast and a keen model engineer, who at one time owned a $2\frac{1}{2}$-ton model of a Stirling Single and who had largely built by hand a model of a GN Atlantic. This was the time, too, when some redoubtable railway photographers began their activities, such as F. E. Mackay and H. Gordon Tidey.

The last two decades of the nineteenth century saw real developments in railway literature — books and periodicals, the latter offering the most progress towards a railway hobby. A technical monthly magazine such as the *Railway Engineer*, which was first published in February 1880, offered the fullest coverage of all new locomotive and rolling stock development to an extent envied today. The pre-grouping railways also clearly used the technical press more effectively than British Rail does today. More general railway journals such as the *Railway Gazette*, first published in 1905, offered intelligent coverage of the considerable railway developments at home and

5

abroad. By 1935 *Railway Gazette* incorporated not only *Railway News* but also *Railway Record, Railway Official Gazette, Railways Illustrated, Transport, Herapath's Railway Journal*, the *Railway Times*, and in that year had absorbed *Railway Engineer*.

But these were principally for professionals and interest now centred on two new monthly magazines which were of more direct value to the railway enthusiast. First came *Moore's Monthly Magazine* from January 1896, associated with the formation of Locomotive Publishing Co, to be a fount of publications and products for the semi-technical railway enthusiast market. The famous address of 3 Amen Corner, London EC4, together with F. Moore's high-quality coloured prints and postcards, deserve fuller coverage than we can give them here. A mixture of a professional and enthusiast approach characterised LPC's magazine which became the *Locomotive Magazine* from January 1897. Continuing into the 1950s, despite being bombed out of its old publishing address, LPC was purchased by Ian Allan Ltd in 1956. The *Locomotive, Carriage and Wagon Review*, ex-*Moore's*, ex-*Locomotive*, ceased publication in November 1959.

Still 'not out' is the *Railway Magazine*, the first truly railway enthusiast magazine which appeared in July 1897. This appealed to professional railwaymen, as well, and early issues were concerned with the railways' commercial and financial affairs.

Cause or effect, but the *Locomotive* and *Railway Magazines* featured several excellent writers on railway matters, nearly all one-time or current railway employees with an ability to write well and careful to be accurate. Charles Rous-Marten, the Rev W. J. Scott, Ernest Leopold Ahrons and Cecil J. Allen all deserve more detailed character sketches than can be given here, but a few facts are relevant and interesting. Rous-Marten and the Rev Scott wrote in *Railway Magazine* from the first issue and with their close knowledge of railway operations of the 1880s and 1890s, including the Races to the North, they must have contributed greatly to the success of the magazine. E. L. Ahrons, born 12 August 1866, left college to be a pupil under William Dean from 1885-88. He moved into general industry and went abroad, to return to England in 1898 and became a frequent contributor to the *Locomotive* from 1903. His great memorial was the definitive study, the *British Steam Railway Locomotive 1825-1925*, published in 1927.

C. J. Allen, born 1886, entered the service of the Great Eastern Railway in 1903 and continued in railway employment thereafter. From August 1909 (and until 1959) he contributed the *Railway Magazine* feature *British Locomotive Practice and Performance*, at first quarterly, then monthly.

Both these men were a mixture of professional railwaymen and enthusiast and made a considerable contribution to the development of the railway hobby. Of course, it couldn't have been difficult to be interested in railways in their heyday before World War 1. Backed by the growth of railway publishing and the interest in photography, much of the foundation of what we take for granted in the enjoyment of railways was laid in the Edwardian era.

After World War 1 and railway grouping, there was a surge in interest in railways, helped by the careful nurturing of that interest by the Big Four's publicity and public relations departments. The appearance of big, powerful express passenger locomotives, the Gresley 'A1' Pacifics, LMS 'Royal Scots', Southern 'Lord Nelsons' and GWR 'Castles' and 'Kings' was a major influence, no doubt. The GWR produced the W. G. Chapman railway books for boys and with excursions to Swindon Works and talks to schools astutely fanned the flames of popular enthusiasm for locomotives and new railway developments. More generally, there were important events such as the trial of the 'Castles' on the Euston-Crewe and Kings Cross-Leeds main lines, the exhibition of locomotives at the Wembley 1924 Exhibition and, of course, the Stockton and Darlington Railway Centenary Celebrations of 1925. The popular newspapers of the day seldom failed to give star treatment to new locomotives; all told, a generation was brought up to glory in railways.

With this sort of background, national railway societies now started to make ground and develop the hobby. The Railway Correspondence and Travel Society was founded nationally in January 1928 (having its beginnings in a Cheltenham-based group the previous year). The Society was something different. Despite the amount of railway literature, accurate details of locomotive allocations, workings and the like were not freely available. The RCTS set out to make this information available to its members and from May 1928 started a monthly journal providing a continuous record of railway happenings. The Society developed a programme of visits, meetings and lectures and like the SLS, too, started to extend its activities to look at overseas railways. A real milestone came on 11 September 1938, when the RCTS ran the first ever main line railtour with Stirling 4-2-2 No 1 and seven ECJS six-wheelers from King's Cross to Peterborough — 170 seats at 5/- (25p) each!

The railway companies extended their involvement in publishing by the appearance in 1927 of E. T. Macdermot's *History of the Great Western Railway*, published by the Railway, and C. F. Dendy Marshall's *History of the Southern Railway and its Constituent Companies*, in 1937, published by the SR.

But these two monumental tomes were for the

academic side of the hobby; the real growth in the railway hobby came through the excitement associated with the LMS and LNER's 'streamliners' of the 1930s, the withdrawal of many famous Victorian classes of locomotive and the fact that there was now a wide range of proprietary model railway equipment available, with the appearance in the late 1930s of Trix and Hornby-Dublo 'OO' gauge electric trains. Right at the end of the period came a new railway magazine, *Railways*, a pictorial periodical featuring the prototype and model railways. First published in 1939, it later became *Railway World*.

But there were no inexpensive lists of locomotives on sale, the sort of books to allow youngsters the chance to learn something about locomotives and lead them to take the railway hobby seriously. Ian Allan joined the Southern Railway in 1939 in the General Manager's office. One of his tasks was to deal with the many enquiries relating to the Southern's locomotive fleet and to save work he suggested that the Company should publish a cheap and handy booklet listing its stock. The SR didn't take up Ian Allan's proposal but it did agree to the booklet being published as a private venture. In 1942 *The Abc of Southern Locomotives* appeared — 2,000 copies being printed — and was put on sale at one shilling (5p). In time the Abcs covered all the 'Big Four' locomotive fleets, and other transport subjects too. Ian Allan Ltd became synonymous with the publishing of a wide range of inexpensive, attractive, well-illustrated transport publications aimed, for the most part, at a younger audience — the present writer being a good example. Railway publishing had entered the mass market.

To back it up Ian Allan ran railtours to the railway works and before long more and more societies were formed to run meetings and organise shed visits, such as the Locomotive Club of Great Britain, in 1949. Other societies specialised in railtours over little-used lines, behind unusual motive power and steadily became more ambitious as steam power vanished from the scene and branch lines closed. From the 1960s overseas railtours were becoming a feature, too.

From being spectators, railway enthusiasts had now become participants and the story of railway preservation is a huge topic on its own. The pioneer was the SLS which had privately preserved the London, Brighton & South Coast Railway 0-4-2 *Gladstone* way back in 1927. From a locomotive to a railway, the Talyllyn, which was taken over by the Preservation Society in 1951. Then the Festiniog, 1955; the Welshpool & Llanfair, 1959, and now the first standard gauge preservation projects were opened for passenger traffic, the Middleton Railway and the Bluebell Railway, both getting under way in 1960.

All this was associated with an explosion in railway publishing, helped by the Indian Summer of steam in the late 1950s and the huge range of new motive power ushered in under British Railways' Modernisation Plan of 1955. We should not forget the emergence of the railway hobby on to the tv screen during the mid/late 1950s with BBC tv's *Railway Roundabout*.

Then came a possible watershed. With Beeching and the rundown of the railway system and the end of steam, would the hobby follow suit and fade away? Certainly, some publishers thought so, even as they contemplated the whirlwind of last trains, farewell appearances by famous steam classes and the hectic, if artificial, atmosphere of 'steam-chasing' in 1967 and 1968.

Once steam finished in August 1968, and with it the end of steam railtours, shed visits and all the familiar atmosphere of the postwar railways, some societies did lose membership and sales of railway publications suffered a little.

But within a year or so of something like a vacuum the hobby changed, became more sophisticated and diversified. There were probably four directions. Some 'steam men' set off on a last chase of non-BR steam in pursuit of the final months of some of the major steam-worked industrial systems. The 'main liners' merely looked 20 or so miles across the Channel and revelled in the exploits of SNCF Pacifics out of Calais and Boulogne, then went further afield in Western and Eastern Europe. With the death of BR steam, coincidentally the preservation movement 'took off'

Below: Train spotters of the late 1940s, in action in a Waterloo-Portsmouth emu.

with the establishment of major standard gauge projects such as the Severn Valley and North Yorkshire Moors Railway and steam centres like Carnforth and Dinting. Another section of the enthusiast movement stuck with BR and widened its interest to cover the disappearance of doomed diesel locomotive classes, the melting away of the 1930s Southern Railway multiple-units and diversified into rolling stock and signalling.

As the 1970s progressed, the railway hobby saw no bounds to its expansion, but what has happened is still fresh in our minds and now part of the accepted scene: the return to main line steam on BR; enthusiasts chasing steam to the ends of the globe, money no object; more and more ambitious private railway operations; 'big events' like Shildon, 1975, and Rainhill, 1980.

The more immediate signs are clear. Railway publishing has gone from strength to strength. More and more titles have appeared, there is a vast range of pictorial albums and a strong growth in magazine circulations, some of which have quadruped since the early 1960s.

Perhaps the railway hobby has reached maturity. It has stabilised, consolidated and everyone seems relatively satisfied. There are signs of a renewed interest in local railway societies, a heartening demand for higher quality historical railway modelling and a growth in the study of the historical and industrial archaeological aspects of railways. British Rail has decided to work with the railway hobby to the mutual benefit of the owners of preserved main line steam and the private railway companies. On BR itself, the gradual standardisation of motive power and rolling stock shows no signs of dampening the attraction of railway operations. Perhaps Rainhill and Rocket 150 will give us some clue to the railway hobby of the 1980s, but with a flourishing private railway sector it seems set for a happy and successful future. What a long way we have come from professional societies and institutions for career railwaymen!

Below: Farewell to steam: cameras at the ready as 'Castle' 4-6-0 No 4079 *Pendennis Castle* backs on to the Ian Allan high-speed Paddington-Plymouth railtour of 9 May 1964.

Walkden

DAVID N. CLOUGH BA

Today there are few surviving industrial railway systems. The move to road as the principal form of freight haulage has rendered redundant many such internal networks. This run-down of rail facilities, particularly in the form of private sidings connected to the national network, is a situation that Government grants to industrial users under Section 8 of the Railways Act, 1974 aim to reverse. Time was, however, when such systems were quite common. Docks, coalfields and power stations were the main locations but large works occasionally warranted their

existence. Such an example would be the Bowater Paper Company's system in Kent, part of which is now preserved as the Sittingbourne & Kemsley Light Railway. Of the ones surviving perhaps the best known are the NCB examples in South Wales, one or two of which happily retain steam operations. Not so fortunate as these was the group of lines that once centred on Walkden, just west of Manchester, for these are now no more than a memory. The collieries that formed their *raison d'etre* have all long since been closed.

Coal mining has a long history in that part of the world. The land was part of the estates of the Dukes of Bridgewater. They had achieved their rank as a result of the legal skills displayed by Sir Thomas Egerton, the illegitimate son of Squire Egerton of Cheshire, during the reign of Elizabeth I. When James I came to the throne, Egerton was elevated to Lord Chancellor and became Baron Ellesmere, declining the rank of Earl. His son was more disposed to this idea and after a

Below: The ex-North Staffordshire Rly 0-6-2T repainted in NSR livery lifts coal to the Sandhole Washery in April 1965, with 0-6-0T *Charles* banking.   *W. J. V. Anderson*

suitable payment in the right quarter he was created First Earl of Bridgewater. His grandson was raised to the status of First Duke and it was his son who became the Third, and last, Duke of Bridgewater who gained fame through his sponsorship of the construction of the Bridgewater Canal.

As a result of the high charges levied by the Irwell Navigation Company for the conveyance of the coal from his mines the Third Duke was spurred into achieving the allegedly impossible task of constructing a canal. To this end, the technical assistance of James Brindley, an unlettered man whose engineering genius is beyond question, was the most significant factor. The canal started at Worsley Delph and no doubt provided the impetus for the establishment at nearby Patricroft of the Bridgewater Foundry. This later became Nasmyth, Wilson & Company Limited and was well-known as a locomotive builder.

Though keen on canals, a trait originating from his appreciation early in life of the Languedoc Canal which joined the Bay of Biscay to the Mediterranean, the Third Duke was none too keen on 'tramroads'. On his death the vast estate was divided up and the mines and the canals went into trust under the control of Robert Haldane Bradshaw. The income from the trust went to the Marquis of Stafford, later to become the Duke of Sutherland and also the First Earl of Ellesmere. It was the spiralling charges made by Bradshaw, for the Duke had always charged reasonable rates, that provoked local merchants into the promotion of a railway between Liverpool and Manchester. Stafford did not approve of the high tariffs and metaphorically cut his own throat by subscribing £100,000 to the construction of the railway. At this time the Canal was earning revenues of this amount annually. If Bradshaw had adopted a more enlightened approach, the construction of the Liverpool and Manchester would have been postponed for some ten years or more.

Meanwhile, despite the reduction in the prosperity of the Canal, the collieries continued to expand with the increasing appetite for coal from a Manchester that was becoming more and more industrialised. The late 1920s saw the merging of the Bridgewater collieries, centred on the workshop facilities at Walkden, which with other colliery owners in the area were to form Manchester Collieries. Included in the new consortium were pits east of Manchester on Ashton Moss and those formerly owned by the Fletcher Burrows' and Arthur Knowles around Atherton and Tyldesley, also to the west of Manchester. The last had their own system of railway lines based on Gin Pit where workshop facilities were retained; all other locomotive servicing was carried out at Walkden.

By now all the former Bridgewater collieries had been connected by rail. A line had been constructed

Top: 0-4-0WT No 3 at Atherton Colliery in 1906, a locomotive built by Hawthorns & Co of Leith in 1867. *A. Leather*

Centre: Two ex-NSR 0-6-2Ts pass at Mosley Common on 3 September 1960. Left is *Kenneth*, right is *Princess*, as repainted for the Stoke Jubilee celebrations. *W. S. Darby*

Above: Hudswell Clarke Austerity 0-6-0ST *Harry* (1776 of 1944) eases loaded wagons over a canal bridge by Astley Green Colliery on 2 March 1970. *David Birch*

from the coalfield down to Worsley permitting some output to go by canal and so continue the practice commenced by the Third Duke. The final link in the system was forged in 1932 when Astley Green Colliery, ironically the last to survive, joined the group and a line was constructed to link it to Booths Bank where canal wharf facilities were also available. With this addition, interchange of traffic with the London, Midland & Scottish was now possible on Astley Moss on the former Liverpool & Manchester line, at Ellenbrook & Sanderson's Sidings, Worsley, on the Tyldesley branch, at Walkden High Level & Cleworth Hall to the ex-Lancashire & Yorkshire Atherton line and on Linneyshaw Moss on the Manchester to Bolton route.

Nationalisation of the coal industry in 1947 had little impact as far as the railway system and workshops were concerned. Gin Pit and further west, Haydock, on the NCB system near St Helens, each remained responsible for maintaining their own locomotives, as also did Kirkless depot at Wigan. Rationalisation in the 1960s resulted in Kirkless concentrating on the repair of coal-face machinery while Walkden now serviced locomotives not only from Lancashire, but also Cumbria and North Wales. The other two depots closed as, apart from all else, the collieries on their systems had succumbed due to low productivity. This is the situation today, although only two collieries now retain steam in the Walkden service area, Bickershaw and Bold, and regular steam working at the former ceased in February 1979.

Motive power on the system has had a varied pedigree. Nasmyth Wilson supplied some units, as did Sharp, Stewart and Hunslet Engine Co. A War Department tank was purchased after World War I and five ex-North Staffordshire Railway 0-6-2Ts were obtained from the LMS, the last one arriving on 8 October 1937. The builder's plates on these five showed construction to have been in 1923 although it is believed to have been a little earlier than this. One of them, ex-LMS No 2271, later named *Princess*, was borrowed by British Rail in 1960 for the City of Stoke Jubilee celebrations, being exhibited at Stoke station. For the event it was repainted at Crewe Works in North Staffordshire livery and retained these colours on returning to Walkden. Happily it has been preserved at the Staffordshire County Museum, Shugborough Hall, Great Heywood.

Below: Walkden loco shed on 3 August 1964. Outside are: *Warrior* (HE 3778/52); *Revenge* (HE 3699/50); *Wasp* (HE 3808/54). In the right background is ex-NSR 0-6-2T *Kenneth.* H. A. Gamble

No new locomotive construction was ever undertaken in the workshops, although spares were manufactured, especially as the demise of many of the original builders would otherwise have made them unobtainable. The neighbouring Gin Pit system employed three 0-8-0Ts, a type rare in British industrial usage. In 1930, one of these, believed to be *Kathrine*, was tried out on the Walkden system for six months, with a locomotive from there going in exchange to Gin Pit. Apart from this short trial these engines spent their working lives on their native metals. This localised approach to allocations was generally true for the other systems and at Walkden engines would be based at one particular colliery or on a stretch of line for long periods.

After World War 2 purchases were almost exclusively of Austerity-type 0-6-0STs, their inside motion being less exposed to the dirt that proliferates at any colliery. Engines were always turned out so that their chimneys faced uphill to minimise the risk of priming. Although the number of engines employed on the system varied from time to time, in the heyday of the lines between 12 and 14 were required to cope with the traffic.

Most locomotives were named, and before the creation of the National Coal Board these were generally in honour of the colliery owners and their families. The 'Knotty' (ex-NSR) engines acquired regal titles due, no doubt, to the timing of their purchase in the mid-1930s. After World War 2 nomenclature with a military flavour took over.

The original livery used on the colliery locomotives was black with gold lining on the tanks and cab. Individual styles continued for some while after state control, with engines from other systems being repainted after overhaul in colours indigenous to their native system. In later days a maroon scheme with gold lining-out was generally adopted.

When the collieries were still connected to BR, engines from within the Lancashire area could come to Walkden for repair under their own steam. In recent years road transport has had to be used. Visits to shops were usually made every 2½-3 years. But there were no running powers over BR for Walkden locomotives to work trains.

Until the rationalisation of workshop facilities that took place in the 1960s, locomotive allocation was Walkden's responsibility. More recently this function has been carried out by the Plant Pool at the NCB Divisional Headquarters in Stoke. In the heyday of the system each driver was allocated his own engine. Apprentice railway workers commenced duties in the sidings before progressing to firemen, brakesmen and drivers. It was common practice for the fireman to act as an additional brakesman as many of the routes included steep gradients.

There was an interesting development in the 1950s with the fitting of Giesl ejectors to several locomotives. *Wasp* was fitted with a Hunslet-pattern device and also received a Kylphor underfeed stoker. The move came partly as a response to smoke control regulations in urban areas and also as an attempt to reduce coal consumption. Trials were carried out on test trains and it was found that coal consumption was reduced by about 10%, combined with a marginal enhancement in performance. Unfortunately, lack of capital precluded large-scale conversion of locomotives. Austerity tank *Respite*, now at Bickershaw Colliery, still has a Giesl ejector fitted and it would be interesting to know if this was the last remaining engine in revenue-earning service outside preservation hands in Britain with such a device. Sister engine *Repulse*, which is similarly fitted, is now preserved on the Lakeside & Haverthwaite Railway.

The old colliery-owners had their own fleets of coal wagons. Manchester Collieries built some of their own at Walkden. Later nearly all were sold off to the Central Wagon Co, Wigan, and today the only NCB-

Right: Industrial steam still lingered on into the 1980s. On the National Coal Board's Mountain Ash, Mid-Glamorgan system, Peckett 0-6-0ST *Sir Gomer* (1859 of 1932) banks a diesel hauled train on 25 May 1979. *P. J. Robinson*

Industrial steam

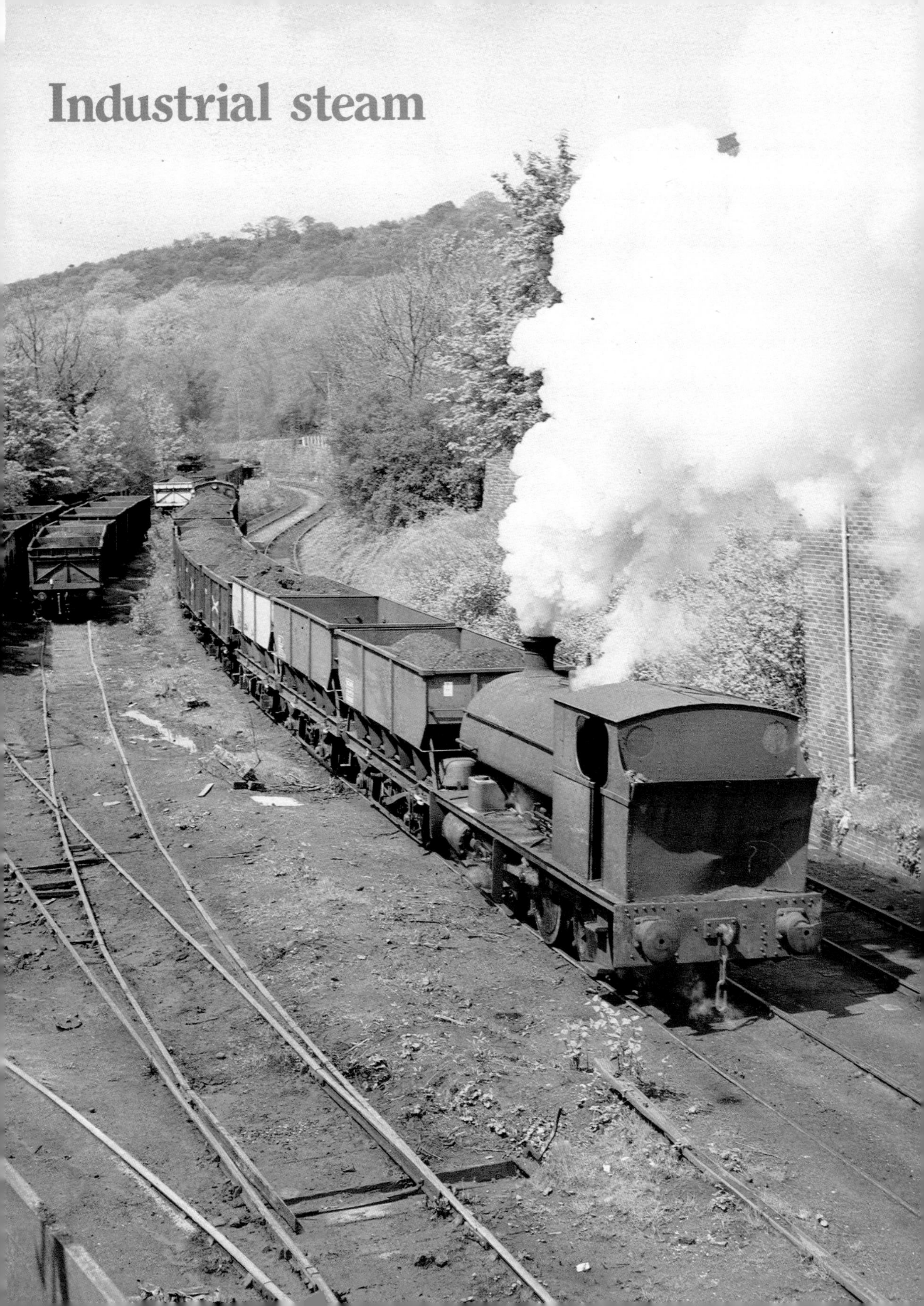

owned wagons surviving are confined to the colliery yards. Unlike some of the more sophisticated systems elsewhere no provision was ever made for signalling on any of the lines. The movement of traffic was controlled by telephones at strategic points.

The Canal Duke had been a benevolent if not overly generous employer. He had provided reasonable housing as well as a library for his employees. This attitude towards welfare was continued by succeeding employers in the provision of a passenger service from Ashton Field to both Sandhole and Mosley Common pits. In the days before adequate local public transport existed it could prove difficult for workers to get to the pitheads on time. To alleviate this problem several passenger carriages were purchased from the LMS to provide a service to work in the morning and home again at night. This continued until about 1932 when buses took over.

In the 1950s and 60s enthusiasts' specials were operated over the system, travelling to Worsley Wharf, Brackley and Astley Green. Two of the 'Knotty' engines, the restored *Princess* and *Sir Robert* were favourites on such turns. In recent years Walkden

Left: At NCB Bedlay Colliery, Glenboig, Strathclyde, Barclay 0-4-0ST No 17 (2296 of 1950) shunts on 13 September 1979. *Bob Avery*

Below: Mossley Green Colliery on 18 January 1962. Austerity 0-6-0ST *Charles* (HC 1778/44), newly fitted with a Giesl ejector, is hard at work. Right is an ex-NSR 0-6-2T. *J. R. Carter*

workshops have given valuable assistance and advice to several preservation societies. A set of drawings for a Giesl ejector was supplied to a Staffordshire preservation group to enable them to fit such a device to one of their locomotives. Certain servicing equipment has been supplied to the Lakeside & Haverthwaite Railway and some repairs have been carried out for the Keighley & Worth Valley Railway, Dinting Railway Centre and Steamport, Southport.

Several locomotives that either worked at Walkden or were serviced there have survived the cutter's torch. *Princess* has already been mentioned. The Worth Valley have Lancashire & Yorkshire 0-6-0ST No 752, a tank which worked at Parsonage, as well as Robert Stephensons & Hawthorn Austerity 0-6-0ST *Fred* from Walkden. A local coal merchant also owns a Hudswell Clarke Austerity 0-6-0ST called *Harry*.

The system had a good safety record. On one occasion, however, a runaway occurred, the delinquent train ending up in the grounds of Walkden public baths! Now the entire network has been lifted. Environmental improvement schemes and road construction have obliterated most of the routes. As mentioned earlier, Astley Green colliery was the last to close, in 1969, with steam being used on demolition trains into 1970.

Thanks must go to Mr J. J. Cunliffe, Works Superintendent at Walkden Workshops, for sparing the time to relate the system's history and to Adrian Davies of Manchester Central Library for assisting me in obtaining information on the Bridgewater family.

A tale of two trains

DEREK CROSS

This is not an attempt to recreate a Race to the North although in many ways the current policies of the East Coast and the West Coast routes to Scotland have more than a hint of the racing spirit of 1895. There is also a throwback to the LNER/LMS rivalry of the 1930s with the East Coast going to relatively frequent light trains and the West Coast sticking to heavier, if less frequent services. The supreme irony of this situation is that in the late 1930s it was Sir Nigel Gresley's rejection of the German 'Flying Hamburger' fast diesel multiple-unit concept that led to the 'A4s' and the 'Silver Jubilee' 'Coronation' and 'West Riding' streamliners and yet, in 1978, the coming of the Inter-City 125 units (ICI25s) to the East Coast main line gave the Kings Cross-Edinburgh service exactly what the German trains would have been had Gresley not rejected them. By contrast, the West Coast route with its tradition of heavy, if more easily timed, trains survived into the 1970s and the coming of electrification, albeit with more frequent services than in steam days.

At the time I am writing, the West Coast's Advanced Passenger Train is still in the testing stage. Through the kindness of the Scottish, Eastern and London Midland Regions of BR I was privileged to ride in the cabs of the representative trains on both the East

Above: The diversions arising from the Penmanshiel Tunnel collapse saw Inter-City 125s and West Coast electric locomotives working side by side, such as at Carstairs on 7 July 1979, with a Class 81 on a down West Coast train and an IC125 waiting to work to Edinburgh. *C. J. M. Lofthus*

Coast and West Coast routes in the autumn of 1978 and the late spring of 1979 respectively. It provided a fascinating comparison. While all comparisons are odious and I don't like making them, in an article of this nature I will in the end be forced to do so. However, before trying to sum up the relative merits of both routes and their crack passenger trains, let me try to describe the journeys in some detail, as seen from the cab — in the case of the East Coast from the train itself.

My first journey was on the 15.10 from Edinburgh (Waverley) to Kings Cross of 9 August 1978 when I travelled in the cab from Edinburgh to Newcastle of the IC125 set numbered 254.013, with power cars Nos 43.080 and 43.079 respectively. On the East Coast main line IC125s carry two fully qualified drivers, in my case Messrs A. Sidley and J. Cooper, both of Gateshead, and a Scottish Region Inspector, Jack Liddle, accompanied me in the cab. It was to prove an interesting and impressive journey, and one very different from anything I have seen from the operative end of a train before. My first impression of the IC125 cab was that it was not a train at all, but an aircraft. The controls, gauges and speedometer were more akin to an aeroplane than a train, only the braking arrangements owed something to standard railway practice as we used to know it. Even here there was a difference in that the brakes were not applied at very high speeds except in an emergency; where possible speed was allowed to slacken on approaches to stations before the brakes were actually applied. This was to save excessive wear on the brake pads which had become evident on the Western Region's IC125s with their more frequent station stops as compared with the East Coast main line. Another notable feature on a first acquaintance with the cab of a IC125 was the lack of noise. Even the LMR electrics had a distinct noise level whereas our IC125 was so quiet that normal conversation was possible even at maximum power. Like the rest of the train the driving cabs are air-conditioned and another feature that struck me was that the guard is in touch with the loco crew by phone and there is no blowing of whistles or waving of green flags at starts from stations, simply a call to the driver that it was time to be off. Promptly at 15.10 we ghosted out of Waverley and into Carlton Hill Tunnel. The start was so quiet and unassuming that it took a second look at the speedometer to realise that we were already in the 60s by the time we passed the site of the old St Margarets loco depot. Some years before I had travelled in the cab of an LMR electric out of Euston and watched fascinated as a set of miniature traffic lights jumped up and down between green, yellow and red indications that the locomotive was overloading. I commented on this to Inspector Liddle who laughed and said I was obviously an LMS man with out of date ideas as the power/weight ratio of the IC125s was such that you couldn't overload them: this was to be vividly demonstrated some forty minutes later.

The journey across the first stage of the market gardening plains of East Lothian was unremarkable other than the fact that it was being done at about twice the speed that I had last known from the cab in steam days. One remarkable feature was the realignment of Monktonhall Junction which I knew well as a schoolboy playing truant to watch the trains go by and then, in later years, with a camera. The East Coast route has now been realigned to take the westernmost bridge over the River Esk that was formerly used only by coal trains to Smeaton and points on the plateau of East Lothian beyond. One result of this has been the imposition of a 60mile/h restriction round the curves in place of the previous 70 but it did give me the most graphic example of the powers of acceleration of an IC125. No sooner were we off the curves than the throttles were opened full out and within a mile the

Above: IC125 journey. Unit 254.013 at Edinburgh Waverley on the occasion of the author's trip. *Author*

Below: The view ahead on Cockburnspath bank, on the occasion of the author's footplate ride. *Author*

train was at the line maximum of 100mile/h, no noise, no fuss, no apparent bother. Then came two of the fascinating throwbacks of railway history. First we passed the station of Prestonpans, still used by stopping trains to North Berwick; not far from Prestonpans, at St Germains, was the only manually operated level crossing between Edinburgh and North Berwick. At first sight this seems an anachronism but, after the Hixon disaster near Stoke on Trent in the late 1960s, St Germains crossing has been retained deliberately as the turn-out on to the main road is such that a long and heavy lorry could foul the running lines if it had to wait to join the main road.

The other interesting railway story of Prestonpans is that here was probably the first use of a railway in the history of warfare. During one of the Stuart rebellions, I think in 1715, there was a tramway from a pit in the hills to a port on the coast near Prestonpans. Under the command of General Cope the English Army had rashly camped astride this tramway before marching on Edinburgh. At an early hour the Scots let loose a rake of loaded coal wagons from the top of the incline and these crashed through the English camp, causing much confusion among the sleeping soldiery, and I believe some casualties. It also gave rise to a song well-known for many years in South Scotland: 'Hey Johnny Cope, are 'ye waking yet'... it also caused a

precipitate withdrawal of the English troops to regroup about Dunbar. Dunbar is also a changed place with the main line avoiding the station to the west and there there is the strange, almost surrealist passage of Oxwellmains cement complex where everything is coated in white, like a bad early horror film.

So far on my journey things had gone well with only a slight loss of time on account of a permanent way restriction near Drem but Nemesis was not far away. Right at the bottom of the climb to Cockburnspath there was a dead stand for signals at Innerwick. There could have been better places to stop although one of our drivers said that it would have been a grand excuse to fill the boiler in steam days. But this check was in fact caused by a signal failure as the new power box at Waverley had not long been installed and there were still some 'bugs' in the system. Once clear there was no hesitation. The throttles were opened wide and the train leapt forward up the 1 in 96 of the once dreaded Cockburnspath Bank. This was probably the most dramatic example of the power and adhesion of the IC125. There was no question of slip, according to the crew there was no such possibility, and we went up the bank like the proverbial rocket even with a train of nearly 416 tons. So much so that power had to be shut off for the 60mile/h limit through the ill-omened Penmanshiel Tunnel that was to fall in with tragic results some months later on 17 March 1979, never to be re-opened. It was a startling example of power unleashed and with the interlinked throttles it was all done with no apparent effort though I was told that both the leading and trailing power cars were on their best behaviour on my behalf. Alas, this energy was in vain as we were stopped for some six minutes while a torpid Class 40 stowed its train into the refuge sidings at Grantshouse.

This was a hint of what was to come in Northumbria. Although the technicians have produced what is a very fast and potent train indeed, these attributes do not describe the mentality of those operating the signalling and control. Perhaps this is unfair as the Waverley power box had only been in operation for a matter of weeks, but it made me wonder as some six months later I had the same experience on the West Coast main line when the 'Royal Scot', already running late, was delayed by what can be most kindly ascribed as an error of judgement by the box at Motherwell. On that occasion the Inspector's comments, alas, cannot be repeated but the drift of them was that they have had the thing for two years and can't work it yet.

There can be little doubt that the final miles along the coast from Burnmouth to Berwick are scenically among the most attractive in the country with the line hugging the cliffs above the sea. I was lucky as by now it was a sunny afternoon although the crew assured me

that earlier in the week visibility had been a matter of a few hundred yards on account of mist drifting off the sea. The Berwick stop was carried out swiftly, but despite the recovery margins and spirited running where possible north of the Border, our departure was a little late. Then came one of the most interesting parts of the whole run, if one of the most depressing. The old North Eastern line through Northumbria simply was not ready for IC125s. Time and again we experienced checks when approaching manual level crossings and could see the signalman frantically winding his wheel to open the gates while we got yellows; clearly, manual level crossings and IC125s didn't mix. So archaic was the working on this section that it would not have surprised me in the least to have seen the *Rocket* approaching on the down line with what were known 150 years ago as 'chaldrons' of coals. Still, for all this, we managed to keep near enough time which speaks wonders for the recuperative power of the IC125s despite the numerous slowings for manual level crossings, a dead stand of two minutes at Alnmouth and a very severe 20mile/h slowing for permanent way works at Morpeth. It was only when seen from the cab of 254.013 that I realised just how sharp the curve at Morpeth was, though I cannot see the need for it in the first place.

This section of the run was made most interesting by the reminiscences of the 'Geordie' crew who once over the Border seemed less inhibited in the presence of a Scottish Region inspector. Driver Cooper asked me out of the blue if I had known the Border Counties line from Hexham to Hawick by way of Riccarton Junction. I had to admit that while I had seen parts of it, I had never travelled on it, let alone got any photos. 'Pity', he said, 'you would have got some great photos there. I started as a fireman at Hexham and well remember the 'Scott' class on that road'. He then mentioned some of those stalwart North British 4-4-0s and actually named them, *Jingling Geordie* apparently being one of the most favoured, perhaps on account of its Tyneside associations. It was astonishing to be whisked through the Northumbrian countryside and have the driver of a IC125 regale me with memories of a class of locomotive long extinct on a line long since lifted. Such is the fascination of railways.

While steeped in early railway history, southern Northumberland is hardly the most scenic part of the United Kingdom. Even here there were certain vignettes that fascinated me, one of them grim but compelling, and, as far as I know, never put on record though careful research has proved this improbable story to be true. Some eight miles north of Alnmouth there was a station, long since closed, called Christon Bank. One of the drivers and Jimmy Liddle told me a story about this place that made the hair rise slowly on my scalp. They pointed out a clump of trees to the west of the line and said that this was how the station got its name and that it should have been Christ-on-Bank though this was too much for queasy Victorian stomachs. The reason for this strange name was that when the Newcastle & Berwick Railway was extending towards Berwick, goaded by George Hudson, many of the labourers were Irish and were smitten with some disease, reputed to be either acute influenza or cholera. In the strongly non-conformist north-east they were considered to be infidels and their dead were refused burial in the local parish churchyard, so the Railway Company bought part of a field, had it consecrated and buried the dead navvies there, naming the place for want of anything better, 'Christ-on-Bank'. A strange and rather chilling story for a pastoral part of north-east England, but one which I am sure is true nonetheless and all part and parcel of early railway history, being made all the more extraordinary by being related in the cab of a twentieth century mechanical marvel. The remainder of the run to Newcastle was simply a case of determined driving attempting to offset various annoying and often totally unnecessary delays. The ghosts of Stephenson's chaldrons of coals still clearly stalk Northumbria. The fact that we arrived in Newcastle on time was due in part to some very skilled and determined driving and to the generous recovery margins built into these schedules. A lot has been said of the advantages and disadvantages of recovery margins, but on this trip their justification was demonstrated on the last few

Below: Class 87 No 87.034 *William Shakespeare* (the locomotive on the occasion of the author's footplate trip) speeds through Beattock with the up 'Royal Scot' on 31 March 1979. *D. G. Cameron*

miles into Newcastle where works for the new Metro were at a critical stage near Manors with severe speed restrictions on the main line. This provoked a remark from Driver Cooper that should go down in railway annals as a classic . . . 'They've bored so many holes in Newcastle for the new Metro that in view of the time it is going to take to finish it they are thinking of importing rabbits from Australia to try and get some return on their money'. Who says the glamour of railways is dead? Not I, so long as the astringent humour of drivers can produce cracks like this. It made the long and lovely climb from Hexham up through the Keilder Forest to Riccarton Jn seem very near, though as one who earns his living from the land I would like to add, 'to hell with the rabbits!'

At Newcastle I bid farewell to my friends in the cab and returned to the train for the journey to Kings Cross. This was to be my first ride of any length on a IC125 and I have to admit that I was most impressed, although it was a strange experience to be travelling as a passenger having been in the cab for the last 124 miles. The riding of the stock was superb, as was the standard of catering, all brought to your seat which for somebody with a badly damaged ankle was a treat in itself. I was interested most of all by my table companion, a German, connected I gather with the commercial side of their embassy in London. As we sped southwards and over an excellent meal we got talking. It transpired that he had more than a passing interest in railways and rather put me through my paces as to where we were and why we were there. The historical aspect of the GN/NE main line I coped with fairly well. Where I was nearly beat was that the IC125 covered the ground faster than I had been used to with the

Above: The APT 125 signs in place south of Lamington, in the Clyde Valley, on the West Coast main line, in June 1979.
A. E. Darling

'Tees Tyne Pullman', even if 'A4'-hauled. I was nearly felled as station after station flashed past . . . at IC125 speed you simply could not read the names. Now this may sound silly, but it nearly made me feel silly as when asked where we were I was only saved by a factory at Retford that said it made some form of soap; I was on the point of saying we were at Peterborough. This raises an important point as regards very fast trains. The average station name is totally illegible and, strange as it may seem to planners, people *do* like to know where they are. Along the East Coast main line there are some LNER era signs giving distances, but I think more of these should be introduced outside main stations, with the signs set far enough back from the line to be legible at high speed.

With this one criticism I cannot fault my IC125 trip from Newcastle to Kings Cross. The catering was excellent, the riding equally so, and it clearly made a very favourable impression, not only on my German companion but on a French party opposite. I eavesdropped on them and got the impression that even the crack 'Mistral' did not come up to the standards of the mundane 15.10 Waverley to Kings

Cross. Add to this the fact that we suffered a hailstorm of great ferocity about Stoke Summit, together with some delays round Stevenage, and yet arrived at 'the Cross' on time. There's a lot to be said for Inter-City 125s. And yet, doubts linger and I wonder why? I have called this article *The tale of two trains* and was so kindly allowed to travel in the cab of a IC125. But I have to confess I was slightly sceptical; I arrived at Kings Cross very sure that this was the rail travel of the future . . . it had been fast, comfortable and as seen from the front end the train was an easy master of its task, but was this the answer? Perhaps geologists should not be allowed to trespass on the works and wisdom of engineers, but this is the trait of anyone educated in the natural sciences — we have the disconcerting habit of asking one question . . .*why*?

By kind permission of the London Midland and Scottish Regions I travelled in the cab of the down 'Royal Scot' (10.45 ex-Euston) between Preston and Glasgow. The start was inauspicious since we were 71 minutes late owing to single line working in the Warrington area. With me in the cab were Driver J. Quinn and Inspector George Lawson, the locomotive was Class 87 No 87.034 *William Shakespeare* and there was the normal ten-coach load of Mk3 stock, very full on account of passengers for Edinburgh as the East Coast main line was closed at the time as a result of the Penmanshiel Tunnel disaster. On leaving Preston three things were obvious: this was not the Preston I had known, (the signal gantries so much a feature of that station had gone, as had the vast LNW box immediately north of the station); we had a very good Class 87, not long out of shops, that rode well and accelerated like the proverbial rocket, and in Driver Quinn we had a driver of exceptional ability who was determined, as it proved, not to miss a trick when it came to making up time, even on this very exacting schedule.

The weather over the plains of North Lancashire was dry and bright and remained so as far as Lockerbie. We also had a completely unchecked run, apart from the slowing over the Lancaster curves. The dry rail enabled Quinn to run right up to the line speed limit, but what a changed line it was from when I knew it in the days of steam! Gone were all the LNW boxes, gone was Tebay and most other stations. The only recognisable station, more or less in its original form, was Lancaster and, although Oxenholme and Penrith still had hints of their origins their yards and junctions had vanished into limbo. It was a strange experience to glide at 100mile/h over a line I knew so well and, in a way, rather a sad one. Glide was the right term as No 87.034 rode superbly well. My previous experience in the cabs of electrics had been on Class 86s, some of which were distinctly rough. I commented on this to those in the cab and said that the 87s seemed much better riders and received the cryptic answer . . . 'some of them'. Possibly the most amazing experience of the first part of this journey was the ascent of Shap. We actually had to shut off power for the 90mile/h slowing round the curves at Shap Summit.

The 'Royal Scot' is not booked to stop at Carlisle and this was another strange experience as it was the first time I can remember passing through non-stop.

Actually, we did have a slight check on the approach to the city while the 'Clansman' tucked its tail into the platform, having also been delayed by the trouble at Warrington. From Carlisle to Beattock station was the most splendid piece of track I have ever seen in this country , as it had been up-graded for very high speed tests with the APT. The driver of 87.034 made the best possible use of it, shooting through Beattock station right up to the limit and, if the truth be told, possibly a bit beyond it. This was our undoing, or nearly so, as at Auchencastle a sudden hail shower swept across the line without warning and we slipped *violently* . . . A slip at nearly 100mile/h is alarming to say the least and I don't think I have ever been as frightened when riding on a locomotive in my life. For a few seconds I was sure we were off the road, but this was where Quinn really showed his skill and had things under control so quickly that we still climbed the ten miles of the bank in $6\frac{1}{2}$ minutes. Inspector Lawson told me that this was a fault with the 87s, they had bags of power and speed, but were too light, and under the conditions of a sudden, slippery patch of rail lost their feet. This made me wonder why the concept of the New Zealand articulated 'EW' class electrics has not been taken up in this country, as while fast and powerful these locomotives are also very sure-footed.

Once over the top, the running was more restrained for two reasons. First, the weather was deteriorating rapidly and indeed, even on 25 May, Tinto was white with snow and there was snow lying in patches by the lineside around Elvanfoot. Also, the track with its constant curvature is not in as good condition as the racing ground south of Beattock. In a violent thunderstorm, we made the special stop at Carstairs to let the Edinburgh passengers change into a IC125 that was being used to connect with the Capital, an unusual sight to say the least. For me, the run down the Clyde Valley had been a sad experience as all the charming old Caledonian stations had been demolished with the exception of Thankerton. This seemed such a waste as many of them were of considerable architectural merit, although I suppose a modern railway has to have a modern image. In view of the weather the restart from Carstairs was restrained but, once under way, the acceleration up to Craigenhill was impressive. Nemesis was at hand for Motherwell had let a local stopping emu out in front of us, a habit that is all too common

on this section, as I have found from my own experience as a passenger on the southbound expresses, and which was confirmed with some very pungent comments by driver and inspector.

This checking of expresses by the Glasgow outer suburban traffic is far too common, but it was hoped that the opening of the Argyle line might have relieved it to some extent. Another fact obvious in the final few miles into Glasgow is the difficulty in sighting signals, mainly the result of the lineside vegetation having got out of hand and, in some cases, obscuring signals until they were only a few hundred yards away. Some of the signals are badly sited and get mixed up with background excrescences such as high-rise flats. Apparently this is especially troublesome at twilight but as Inspector Lawson said drily: 'the drivers should ken where to look for them'. I dare say he has a point, but to a stranger it was disconcerting. What was even more disconcerting was the final mile or so into Central where all lines are signalled for running in either direction. Near the site of the old Eglinton Street station I was startled out of my wits by the sight of an emu apparently coming straight for us on the same line. My expression of alarm was greeted by a dry remark from George Lawson that at the next set of points we would go right while the emu went right, then adding, 'with luck'. It smacked of reducing rail safety to 'the thickness of a signal-post'. However, all went well and we duly arrived in Central in one piece having recovered eleven minutes of our late start from Preston. Considering the additional Carstairs stop and the heavily checked run in from Motherwell it was a very creditable effort indeed.

I have titled this article *A tale of two trains*, so what are my conclusions? To this I have to answer that in all honesty I don't really know. There is no doubt that from the point of view of the comfort and convenience of crew and passengers the Inter-City 125 units win. On the other hand, it is obvious that the Class 87s are capable of greater speeds and weight haulage than the present line maximum speed limit allows . . . *if they can keep their feet*. Given this, these locomotives can work flexible train formations depending on the traffic offering at any given time. The IC125s, on the other hand, and the forthcoming APT too, being fixed formations lack the flexibility to meet varying passenger demand, and I have already heard reports of serious overcrowding on the IC125s between Edinburgh and London. But the die is cast for the next few years. Having seen what a Class 87 can do, I feel that the fixed formation train is probably a mistake and that conventional electric locomotives could be developed to run at higher speeds, assuming that the track is up-graded accordingly as it has been on the Carlisle-Beattock stretch. It is also worth pointing out that this is what the German Federal Railways seem to think.

Dugald Drummond's eight-coupled

D. W. WINKWORTH

By the time the Advanced Passenger Train made its first revenue-earning run nearly thirteen years had elapsed since BR publicists first unveiled the concept of such a train to the world at large. This penchant for previewing new developments has evolved over the last thirty years, having had its origin in the announcements made by the 'Big Four' railway companies just before nationalisation when they proclaimed their intended motive power policies.

Previously, a new locomotive design had been shrouded in official secrecy until the machine was completed; despite this, rumours got around and the railway amateur could speculate as to the final shape and specification of the new prototype. For instance, there was the widely-held view that Hawksworth was to abandon some well-established Great Western shibboleths in his 4-6-0 design, which became the 'County' class, some puzzled discussion as to how the Southern electric locomotive, No CC1 of 1941, might bridge third-rail gaps, not a few ideas about the Southern's Pacific design (it would have been a long shot indeed to have got that right!) and, in prewar years, forecasts about the likely features of the LNER 'A4' and its attendant train which were to form the 'Silver Jubilee' train.

Below: First of the 'finds' of drawings was that for the proposed LBSC 0-8-0T — the 'E6' 0-6-2T adapted to carry an extra driving axle. One of the two intended 0-8-0Ts, 'E6' No 32418, at Brighton in 1959. *W. M. J. Jackson*

Recently, now that copies of official locomotive drawings have become available, there has been the opportunity to revive the joy of conjecture. A perusal of one of the lists produced, under the heading LBSC Rly, entries denoting an 0-8-0T with 4ft 6in driving wheels and, more excitingly, an 0-8-0 four-cylinder goods engine. However, speculation did not exactly run riot because the former design was confidently expected to be the Brighton Company's 'E6' class 0-6-2T adapted to carry an extra driving axle — Nos 417/18 had been so earmarked at the time, but eventually appeared as the final members of the 'E6' class — but a four-cylinder eight-coupled design was so unusual for Brighton as to almost defy the imagination.

With the arrival of the copy drawings the tank engine was confirmed as an 'E6' having the trailing wheels substituted by a coupled driving pair and little other in the way of alterations. Braking was not even extended to include the larger wheels.

But the tender engine was another matter. One glance was sufficient to establish that nothing like it had ever come out of Brighton Works. A high-pitched boiler, low-boiler mountings and an elephantine front-end all combined to deepen the doubts that this was an LBSC design at all. Unlike the drawing of the tank engine, this one lacked any mark of origin, such as 'Locomotive Car and Wagon Dept Brighton', having nothing more than a rather obvious title of Four-Cylinder Eight-Coupled Goods Engine.

Having dismissed the proposition that the design was still-born at Brighton, the process of identification was assisted. Safety valve cover, cab design, splasher arrangement and, by no means least, cross-tube firebox all pointed to one of Dugald Drummond's brain-children for the London & South Western Railway. The coupled wheelbase was 17ft 6in, the wheels were of 4ft 10in diameter, and the overall length of frames, 32ft. The four cylinders were $16\frac{1}{2}$in diameter, of 26in stroke with 10in piston valves and were inclined with the drive on to the second and third axles for inside and outside cylinders respectively. Walschaerts valve gear was indicated. The boiler was of 5ft 6in diameter (inside) having a barrel length of

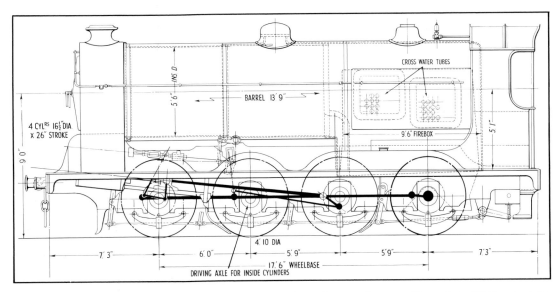

Labels on diagram:
CROSS WATER TUBES
5' 6" INS D
BARREL 13' 9"
4 CYL RS 16½" DIA X 26" STROKE
9' 6" FIREBOX
5' 1"
9' 0"
4' 10" DIA
7' 3"
6' 0"
5' 9"
5' 9"
7' 3"
17' 6" WHEELBASE
DRIVING AXLE FOR INSIDE CYLINDERS

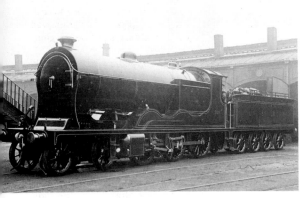

Above: Drummond's proposed four-cylinder 0-8-0 goods engine for the LSWR.

Left: The 0-8-0 derived some features from the LSW 'F13' 4-6-0s, notably the boiler, splashers and cross-water tubes in the firebox. This is 'F13' No 331. *Ian Allan Library*

13ft 9in and a 9ft 6in firebox: the total heating surface of 2,737sq ft was made up of 2,210 for boiler tubes, 357 for the 112 firebox tubes and 170sq ft for the firebox, the grate area being 31½sq ft. No working pressure was shown although this was likely to have been 175lb sq in. The centre of the boiler was pitched 9ft above rail level. The probable weight of the locomotive was in the region of 75 tons.

At the same time that Drummond was trying to arrive at a successful 4-6-0 design it would appear that he considered that more powerful freight locomotives were required and, in so doing, sought to adapt features from six-coupled designs. The boiler was identical with those fitted to the 'F13' class and to the solitary 'E14' of 1907. As the only four cylinder 4-6-0 to have 16½in by 26in cylinders was the 'E14', it would seem that the design for the 0-8-0 was proceeded with during, or after, 1907.

This goods engine would have been a curious amalgam of the 'F13', 'E14' and 'T14' classes. The boiler, as indicated, would have been as the former two classes but the cylinders would have been placed, like the 'T14s', under the smokebox although, unlike the 'T14s' they would be inclined, thereby introducing a heavy-looking front-end. On the other hand, the splasher arrangement owed more to the 'F13' design. The frame was straight with the splashers over the pair of leading wheels being combined with the cylinder casing; the splashers over the second pair of wheels were individual while those over the rear wheels were combined with a straight top to accommodate a sandbox and then swept up to the cab front. The drawing confined itself to the engine but it is unlikely that any tender other than the standard 4,500 gallon type would have been considered for pairing with the locomotive.

Curiously, as has been chronicled elsewhere by Mr C. P. Atkins, Dugald's younger brother, Peter, had propounded an eight-coupled design a few years previously (as a change to his usual process of copying Dugald's designs) for Highland Railway use. At the end of 1902 a drawing was prepared at Lochgorm Works for an inside-cylindered 0-8-0; this clearly indicated that the inspiration for such a machine stemmed from the Caledonian Railway's '600' class of the previous year in that the ungainly wheel-spacing of

Comparative table of selected British 0-8-0 designs

Year	Company	Class	Wheelbase	Driving wheel diameter	Cylinders (No, dia, stroke)	Grate (sq ft)	Heating surface (sq ft)	Boiler Pressure (lb/sq in)	Tractive Effort lb (at 85% BP)	Weight (tons)
1886	Barry	'D'	15ft 5in	4ft 3in	(2) 20in×26in†	22.6	1,440	150	26,000	50½
1901	Caledonian	'600'	22ft 4in	4ft 6in	(2) 21in×26in	23	2,108	175	31,584	60½
1902	GCR	'8A'	17ft 1in	4ft 7in	(2) 19in×26in†	23.6	1,765	180	26,110	61¼
1902*	HR	—	19ft	4ft 9in	(2) 20in×26in	27	2,330	175	N/A	c65
c1907*	LSWR	—	17ft 6in	4ft 10in	(4) 16½×26in	31.5	2,737	175	36,308	c75
1912	LYR	'1546'	16ft 4in	4ft 6in	(2) 21½in×26in	25.6	2,321	180	34,052	66¼
1919	NER	'T3'	18ft 6in	4ft 7¼in	(3) 18½in×26in	26.7	2,427	180	36,963	71½
1921	LNWR	'G2'	17ft 3in	4ft 5½in	(2) 20½in×24in	23.5	2,022	175	28,043	62

* Proposed designs, not built
† Outside cylinders, rest inside cylinders

Above: 'T14' 4-6-0 No 458 provides some clue to the front-end appearance of Drummond's proposed 0-8-0; with this design, however, the cylinders would have been inclined.
W. J. Reynolds/Ian Allan Library

Below: Relatively few pictures exist of the Drummond 4-6-0s on freight trains, such as 'F13' No 331 leaving Salisbury yard with a working to Eastleigh.

that design was followed, although a large boiler was proposed together with crosswater tubes in the firebox.

At the time no other 0-8-0 on British metals came anywhere near Dugald Drummond's LSWR proposal and over a decade passed before it was matched by the North Eastern 'T3' class for size, although doubtless the Darlington product would have outshone the Eastleigh design in the realm of performance. The accompanying table illustrates the dimensional differences between these two designs as well as contrasting those of some other of the twenty or more British 0-8-0 examples which appeared between 1886 and 1921, as well as the proposed Highland essay.

In retrospect, it was perhaps as well that locomotive designers did not give advance publicity to developments in their drawing offices. Fascinating as it would have been to have witnessed one of the monster LSWR 0-8-0s grinding up to Litchfield summit on the Southampton line, it would seem — if the evidence of the Drummond four-cylinder designs which *did* come to fruition is any guide — that the 'H15' class 4-6-0s constructed by Urie in time for the demands of World War 1 constituted a sounder engineering solution.

The 'Clans' at work

For the railway enthusiasts in the south of England the British Railways Standard Class '6' Pacifics, the 'Clans', were great rarities. Today they remain something of an enigma — was the design a failure, or did they do what was asked of them?

This photo feature shows the 'Clans' at work on a variety of workings, other than rail tours which 'cheated' by taking them on to unfamiliar metals.

Above: The 'Clans' spent much time on the Manchester/Liverpool-Glasgow trains. No 72003 *Clan Fraser* near Uddingston on a Glasgow-Liverpool express on 24 July 1952. *E. R. Wethersett/Ian Allan Library*

Right: The 'Clans' might have proved useful in the Highlands. One rare working saw No 72001 *Clan Cameron* on the West Highland Line on 16 June 1956, working a Glasgow-Spean Bridge special and seen here in Glen Falloch. *John Robertson*

Top left: Carlisle Kingmoor shed's 'Clans' worked over the Settle & Carlisle to the end of their lives. On Easter Monday 1963, No 72008 *Clan Macleod* passes Durran Hill, Carlisle, with a Glasgow (St Enoch)–St Pancras relief express. *Peter J. Robinson*

Left: The Kingmoor 'Clans' worked into south-west Scotland. No 72007 *Clan Mackintosh* takes water at Ayr when heading a Stranraer–Newcastle holiday train on 7 August 1965. *Derek Cross*

Top: In September/October 1958, No 72009 *Clan Stewart* was transferred to the Great Eastern Line of the Eastern Region where it was not a success. On 12 September 1958 the engine waits in the bay platform at Liverpool St station. *M. J. Axcell*

Above: No 72005 *Clan Macgregor* is an unusual sight leaving Gloucester Eastgate with a Bristol–Newcastle train in the late 1950s. *T. D. Fry*

Right: No 72005 again, this time heading the 13.40 Llandudno–Derby as it approaches Blythe Bridge on 8 September 1956. *Anthony Cox*

'The Sunset Limited'

J. E. BERRY

All black and white photographs by
S. R. McCombie

Over 2,000 miles of continuous steam haulage behind thirteen different classes of locomotive through some of the most magnificent scenery in South Africa — this was the prospect for the 170 passengers who boarded the 'Sunset Limited' rail tour in Johannesburg station on the evening of 12 April 1979. This unique ten-day rail tour was organised by the Railway Society of Southern Africa as a follow-up to their five-day 'Union Limited/Union Express' from Johannesburg to Cape Town and return in September 1977. The 1979 tour featured steam haulage from Johannesburg to Mossel Bay and return, with travelling mainly by day, the train acting as a mobile hotel supplying all meals and sleeping accommodation at night. The train was sold out long before the day and, in addition to the many South African enthusiasts, carried a sizeable contingent from Britain and the USA. It was made up of eight clerestory-roofed first-class coaches (built in Britain in 1950/51); twin diner No 219 *Protea* (built at Pretoria Workshops in 1933); lounge car No 796 of 1929, half lounge car No 798 (built at Pretoria in 1908) and which was marshalled at the front of the train throughout as a tape-recording 'studio'; a type

'GD23C' guard's van (built Pretoria, 1950), and, lastly, a mechanical refrigerator at the rear to carry supplies. The total weight of this assemblage was 558 tons tare.

At the head of the train at Johannesburg was preserved Class '16E' Pacific No 858 *Allan G. Watson*. The story of the return to service of this fine locomotive in 1977 from storage at De Aar for use on the 'Union Limited' was told in *South African Pacific Survivor* by P. J. Odell (*Railway World*, October 1978). For me the Pacific was one of the highlights of the trip. On my first visit to South Africa in 1972, the '16Es' had just been withdrawn from their final duties on freight work at Bloemfontein and it was disappointing not to have seen one in action. I could not have imagined that seven years later it would be possible not only to see one, but to travel behind it out of Johannesburg. So it was particularly satisfying to accelerate away through the city's suburbs and, later, to sit in the lounge car with a drink and listen to the sound of No 858 working hard up front en route to our first overnight stop at Klerksdorp.

With a pre-dawn departure we awoke to the sound of the '16E' as No 858 effortlessly turned its 6ft driving wheels along the 192 miles to Kimberley where passengers could choose to visit either the famous 'Big Hole' or Beaconsfield locomotive depot with its large allocation of Class '25NC' 4-8-4s and the one or two Class 25 'Condensers' which still survive, if only on shunting duties. From Kimberley haulage of the train was assumed by another preserved engine, Class '16DA' Pacific No 879 (built Henschel, 1930) which De Aar has returned to working order specially for the tour. Looking a splendid sight, she performed most competently on the double-track main line on to

Below left: At the end of the first stage of the 'Sunset Limited', '16E' Pacific No 858 *Allan G. Watson*, on arrival at Kimberley on 13 April.

Above: For the Kimberley-De Aar section, '16DA' Pacific No 879 was provided. The 4-6-2 takes water at Potfontein en route to De Aar on 13 April.

Right: After stabling over the Easter weekend, the 'Limited' awaits departure from Port Elizabeth docks on 16 April behind '15ARs' Nos 2082/2023.

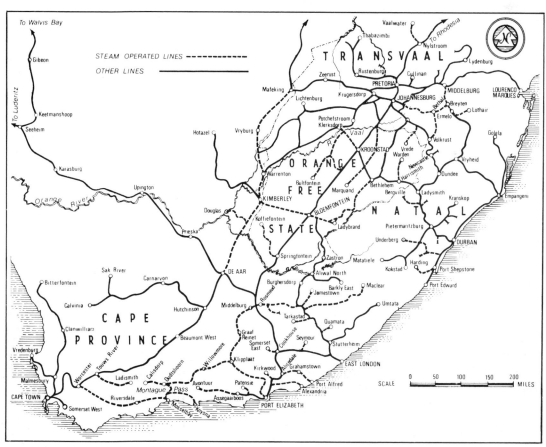

De Aar where the train was welcomed in style by the local brass band. Gleaming in the evening sunshine were Class '12A' 4-8-2 No 1547 and '15A' 4-8-2 No 1970, the famed De Aar pilot *Milly*. The pair took us forward to Noupoort, after an all-too short stop to inspect some of the treasures of De Aar shed. The next morning, No 1547 was in sole charge to Cookhouse where Class '12R' 4-8-2s Nos 1938/1859 backed down for the mainly downhill run to the coast at Port Elizabeth.

There the train was stabled in the dock area over Easter Sunday until mid-morning on Monday to give passengers a chance to visit Sydenham shed and to sample the lively performance of the Class '15AR' 4-8-2s on the suburban service to Uitenhage. On the Sunday, however, most of the 'Sunset Limited's' patrons elected to join a special trip by the 'Apple Express' from the 2ft gauge terminus at Humewood Road to Loerie and be double-headed by a pair of Class 'NG15' 2-8-2s, NG124/NG146. On a beautiful day the highlights of the morning involved a run-past on the highest narrow-gauge railway bridge in the world over Van Stadens Gorge, some 254ft above the river, and the magnificent, eight-mile twisting descent of 647ft down to Loerie. No NG146 turned at Loerie and returned part of the train to Port Elizabeth in time for dinner while No NG124 took three coaches forward on an extension trip up the main line to Gamtoos, then over the 20-mile branch to Patensie with run-pasts to order. There was a minor mishap when NG124 became uncoupled from her train and went racing on ahead to the amusement of the passengers but eventually we were re-united. After viewing the preserved narrow gauge Garratt, No NG81, at Patensie, during which time NG124 was turned and serviced, we set out on the homeward journey arriving back at Gamtoos in the last of the evening sunshine. Then back to Port Elizabeth in the dusk after a magnificent and quite unforgettable day.

We were back on the 3ft 6in gauge the next day and two '15ARs' Nos 2082/2023 took us to the next overnight stop at Klipplaat with some fine sound effects on the climb from Glenconnor. Class '19D' 4-8-2 No 3324 worked alone on the next leg, taking the 'Sunset Limited' through the splendid scenery of the Little Karroo to Oudtshoorn where she was replaced by the unusual combination of Class '24' 2-8-4 No 3652 and Class 'GMA' 4-8-2+2-8-4 Garratt No 4070. The latter sported the name *Amin* on her rear unit because, according to the driver, 'it's big, black and cantankerous!' This pair were in charge for the climb up the northern slopes of the Outeniquas Mountains and then down through the renowned Montagu Pass to George. Class '24' No 3622 trundled us along the Knysna branch as far as Wilderness for the overnight rest. Here we took over the station for the evening and had an impromptu *braaivleis*, or barbecue, on the platform. This came about thanks to electrical difficulties on the dining car *Protea* which had been all too evident in the previous couple of days.

Breakfast the next morning was nonetheless served as usual. 'Usual' is hardly the right way to describe spooning up cornflakes while up front there were treble-headed Class '24' 2-8-4s Nos 3627/669/670. All were in magnificent condition and were in charge for the early morning stage over the remainder of the most beautiful branch line which culminates in a long approach across the lagoon into the terminus at Knysna. There is no doubt that the branch well merits its description as the most scenic line in the whole of South Africa; in addition to the Knysna lagoon there

Below: The 'Sunset Limited' at Snyberg, en route from Klipplaat to Oudtshoorn behind '19D' 4-8-2 No 3324 on 17 April, being passed by sister engine No 3339 on a freight.

Right: The special trip by the 'Apple Express' on 15 April over the 2ft gauge line from Humewood Road to Loerie when the 'Limited's' patrons were hauled by 'NG15' 2-8-2s Nos 124/146. The pair are crossing the Van Stadens Gorge. *J. E. Berry*

Left: A dramatic sight as the three Class '24' 2-8-4s, head the 'Sunset Limited' across Knysna Lagoon on 18 April.
D. C. Williams

Above: The three '24s' on arrival back at George from Knysna on 18 April.

is an ever-changing vista of lake and meadow, woodland and ocean, not forgetting some steep gradients and horseshoe curves. Sufficient, in fact, to keep any photographer happy for weeks! Once at Knysna we had a break of 2½ hours and three choices: a bus trip to The Heads, a (quaintly named) local beauty spot, a walk round the village, or, for those who stayed with the railway interest, the rewarding sights of the three 2-8-4s turning on the triangle and the appearance along the line across the lagoon of Class '24' No 3622 on the morning freight from George. The highlight of the return trip was a run-past on the well-known Kaaimans River bridge which carries the line across an inlet of the Indian Ocean just beyond Wilderness — the sight of the three '24s' blasting across the bridge with their long train was quite something.

And then we were back at George where two Class '14CRB' 4-8-2s Nos 1995/1766 came on to the back of the train having been sent from Cape Town specially. The pair took the 'Limited' down the steep descent to Groot-Brakrivier, passing a couple of 'GMA'-hauled freights en route. and on to Hartenbos, past Voorbaai shed, and on to Mossel Bay where the train was stabled for the night alongside the Indian Ocean. The ailing *Protea* was detached here in exchange for a more modern air-conditioned dining car. Although this made the crew's lives easier, from

the connoisseurs' point of view much of the character of the older vehicle was missing. For the first leg of the homeward journey Nos 1995/1766 retraced their previous day's trip back to George although not without incident. At Groot-Brakrivier No 3652 was provided as banker for the six-mile climb at 1 in 40 up to Outeniekwa. But even with this assistance the '14CRBs' all but came to a stand in the light drizzle which made worse the tortuous curves near the top of the bank; after a superb effort they just managed to keep the train on the move.

'GMA' No 4070 took over again at George and with No 3652 acting as banker, instead of pilot, the Garratt commenced the northbound assault on the Montagu Pass on a line which has severe curves and gradients as steep as 1 in 36. Unfortunately, the scenic beauties of the Pass were lost in the presistent low cloud which made the engines at each end of the train often appear as no more than grey shapes in the murk. Nevertheless the Garratt performed confidently, breasted the summit without difficulty, and then drifted down easily to Oudtshoorn. There side attractions were provided — a visit to a local ostrich farm, and after another open-air dinner on the platform, an evening visit to the beautiful Cargo Caves.

Few of the train's patrons were probably aware of the early departure from Oudtshoorn but awoke on a glorious morning to find two old friends, Class '24' No 3652 and '19D' No 3324, going strong up front. After a photo-stop with the splendid background of the towering cliffs of Toorwaterpoort Gorge, Klipplaat was regained in the early afternoon. Another, different combination of locomotives, '19D' No 3335 and '15AR' No 1788 took charge for the comparatively level and straight stretch to Graaf-Reinet.

'The Sunset Limited' was in the final stages of its tour but still to come was the assault on the Lootsberg Pass, an exhilarating experience and one of the most magnificent steam spectaculars to be found anywhere in the world today. From Graaf-Reinet to Lootsberg summit the line climbs 3,234ft in over 59 miles with an average grade of 1 in 96 but including sections of 1 in 40 on the final ascent from Bethesda Road. This process added up to over three hours of all-out 'thrash' from the locomotives and some fine, rugged scenery. Over the past two or three years, a daily pick-up freight excepted, trains over Lootsberg have been handled by 'GMA' Garratts although, to me, these locomotives do not somehow seem right on this line. The only way to do Lootsberg is with a pair of 4-8-2s and this was what we had on the 'Sunset Limited'. At 07.00, Class '24' No 3617 and '19D' No 3335 left Graaf-Reinet, assisted at the rear for the initial short steep climb by 'GMA' No 4114, a ghostly black shape in the morning mist. The 'GMA' dropped behind, the mist cleared and the two 4-8-2s settled down to their task with a steady roar up to the first water stop at Pretoriuskloof; then on by way of Willow Slopes and

Above: On 18 April, Class '14CRB' 4-8-2s Nos 1995/1766 leave Hartenbos for Mossel Bay with the 'Sunset Limited'.

Right: Ready for the ascent of the Montagu Pass on 19 April, 'GMA' Garratt No 4070 waits with the 'Limited' at George.

Glen Harry with some lively running. Now the noise from twin exhausts took a more urgent note as the engines were driven even harder. After an hour of this a well-earned breather was taken at Koloniesplaas for fire-cleaning and watering and then on once more to Bethesda Road where '19D' No 2672 was waiting to attach as banker and provide assistance for the final 12 miles. Climbing ever higher up the barren hillside the effort never flagged (apart from a photo-stop and run-past that is) and with three exhausts echoing round the mountains we finally topped the summit triumphantly at Lootsberg. The downhill run to Middleburg and Rosmead was something of an anti-climax after all that display but our two locomotives were not quite finished and had a final treat in store. At Rosmead they retired to shed for servicing and returned with a new crew for the 28 miles mainly uphill to

Noupoort. They proceeded to tear up the schedule by cutting the booked 87 minutes timing by 27 minutes. In so doing, they emitted a fantastic volume of noise — more than I have ever heard anywhere else. For sheer 'thrash' value, if nothing else, this run must go unequalled — at one point normal conversation even four coaches back became impossible!

At Noupoort, the 'Limited' bade farewell to the two splendid 4-8-2s and renewed acquaintance with the preserved '16DA' Pacific No 879 which performed very competently with its heavy load over the long stretch of 182 miles via Springfontein to Bloemfontein. Arrival here was just in time to witness the departure of the two overnight passenger trains to Bethlehem and Kimberley, each in the charge of a Class '25NC' 4-8-4.

At last came the final day of the tour and an air of anti-climax was present despite the prospect of haulage by two fresh classes of locomotive. Class '23' 4-8-2 No 3300 worked over the old stamping ground of the class from Bloemfontein to Kroonstad (now electrified) via the famous Karee bank but the locomotive did not seem to be at its best and performed lethargically. From Kroonstad, Class '15CA' 4-8-2 No 2850 took over but produced only spasmodic bursts of action back to Germiston. As steam is banned from running into Johannesburg station we were resigned to electric haulage for the final 9 miles of the tour, but, at least, one of the older electric locomotives was provided in the shape of Class '3E' Co-Co No E194, dating back to 1947.

So ended a truly remarkable rail tour which will doubtless be long remembered by those who were fortunate enough to be on the 'Sunset Limited'. All participants are indebted to the Railway Society of Southern Africa for their foresight in arranging the tour and for the long hours of work involved in its organisation. South African Railways deserve enormous credit for carrying out the progamme with the provision of a succession of locomotives — all magnificently turned out; but never overdone, in typical South African style. Then there was the sterling effort by the train's crew during the ten days of the tour, again a tireless and excellent performance. In short, a probably incomparable experience, envied, no doubt, by scores of steam enthusiasts the world over.

Camping holidays on the railway

R. K. CURRIE

Over the past fifteen years Britain's railways have seen tremendous changes. Steam has given way to diesel and electric traction, the freight traffic pattern is so changed that the formerly well-known, pick-up goods train has virtually disappeared, most branch lines and stations have closed to passengers and freight traffic, while the removal of unwanted sidings and marshalling yards has left many once-important railway centres with little more than Inter-city passengers and parcels traffic. Today's faster main-line travel gives an improved service between the larger centres of population, but there are some once-common railway features whose passing from the scene causes regret.

One departed facility is the camping coach, once to be seen at many stations in the holiday areas of Britain. (Actually, some examples *do* remain but not in BR ownership). According to *Railway Wonders of the World* camping coaches came about when the LNER followed up a suggestion by C. J. Cutcliffe-Hyne, the book's author, and provided ten coaches on their system in 1933. The GWR and LMS followed suit in 1934, the Southern introducing theirs later, and soon there were over 200 camping coaches in use. The outbreak of war necessarily caused the suspension of the scheme, but the coaches became available again soon after the end of hostilities. In 1958, for example, there were 205 coaches on offer, locations ranging from Strome Ferry and Golspie in the far north of Scotland to Corfe Castle in Dorset and from Mundesley-on-Sea in Norfolk to Marazion in Cornwall. Some were situated singly, often in isolated spots, while Squires Gate, Blackpool had as many as fifteen. In the Scottish and North Eastern Regions only, there were camping apartments. Located mainly at stations closed to passengers these apartments were converted from waiting rooms, booking offices and the like to provide accommodation similar to the coaches. The North Eastern Region called their apartments camping cottages. From four to eight persons could be accommodated according to the size of the coach or apartments, although before the war the GWR had at least one coach with ten sleeping berths. At the end of the day the railway camper passed along the corridor and retired to rest either in single beds or in two-tiered bunks. All necessary supplies of crockery and cutlery were provided, together with blankets, pillows, bed linen and tablecloths, the last two items being renewed weekly. The first LMS coaches used in 1934 were let at a slightly higher figure compared with those of the other companies, perhaps because the LMS ones were corridor coaches, while in the case of the others at that time one had to step outside the coach to reach the sleeping compartments. One condition was that return rail tickets from the holidaymakers' home stations to the station where the accommodation was provided or to the nearest station open to passengers must be purchased, and the value of these in revenue was taken into account when the allocations were made.

There was not much difference in the facilities provided in the various coaches apart from those of the Pullman cars converted in the early 1960s, the interiors of which were more spacious. Lighting and cooking were by means of paraffin oil, gas or electricity. Water for all purposes had to be carried in cans from the station premises, toilets being located there too, and these were usually for the exclusive use

of campers. In the case of the apartments and cottages water was sometimes pumped or piped into the accommodation itself, but no hot water was available other than by heating it on the stove. Usually a section of track about a yard in length was removed from the line upon which the coach stood to ensure that the vehicle could not inadvertently reach the running lines.

Our family had a railway camping holiday annually for thirteen years. British Railways recommended that applications for booking should give alternative choices of sites and as we also usually applied to more than one Region, it was quite exciting waiting to see what was offered. We always took the first offer received, however tempting later ones might be. In the months that followed confirmation of the booking, guide books, maps and timetables of the holiday district were studied carefully to make the most of our stay.

We first booked a fortnight at one of the sites in 1953, the choice being Brinkburn camping cottage in Northumberland, on the former North British Railway branch line to Rothbury, closed the previous year to passenger traffic. The station was perched on a hillside in beautiful surroundings, and we occupied the station buildings, which now formed a camping cottage. Paraffin was provided for cooking and lighting, while the water supply was pumped by hand inside the building. One of the blankets bore the legend, 'Edinburgh-King's Cross Fish Services'. The daily goods train delivered our newspaper without stopping and sometimes called to leave our paraffin supply. Ex-NER 'J21' 0-6-0s Nos 65033/35 provided the motive power for these trains, while we had one passenger train during our stay, a 'Cocktail Special' to Rothbury for a private birthday party, calling at stations to pick up and set down guests. 'J21' 0-6-0s Nos 65110/19 double-headed this train.

We travelled about by train and bus in this most attractive county. At the tiny engine shed at Kelso on the line from Berwick-upon-Tweed the only occupants were NBR 'C15' 4-4-2T No 67477 and LNER Sentinel 'Y1' No 68138. An interesting ticket available on this line was the single from Coldstream to Carham, a distance of $5\frac{1}{2}$ miles. Although the ticket appeared to be from Scotland to England, it was actually the reverse of this, for the two railway stations

were located in opposite countries from the communities they served.

Pursuing railway interests further afield, a visit to the National Coal Board at Seaton Delaval provided the stirring sight of the very old outside-framed 0-6-0, No 3 (ex-NER No 658, built 1867), on a long train of coal wagons from New Hartley Pit. Recently repainted at that time the engine made a fine picture with its polished brass safety-valve cover and vermilion-painted coupling-rods glinting in the sunshine. This locomotive was broken up in 1958. By contrast it was sad to find NCB 0-6-0 No 20 being scrapped, the last of the G&SWR tender engines in existence, formerly LMS No 17196.

The South Shields, Marsden & Whitburn Colliery Railway was next visited. Here an 0-6-0ST built in 1952 hauled six-wheeled carriages to provide the passenger service, largely for miners, from Westoe Lane station in South Shields to Whitburn Colliery. We had a ride on this train and at Whitburn Colliery we saw NCB No 8, an ex-NER 'J21' 0-6-0 No 869, which was broken up the following year. Passenger traffic on the line ceased two months after our visit.

During the second week we visited the Lambton Engine Works, Philadelphia, a fascinating place for seeing interesting NCB locomotives. Apart from the very old 0-6-0s, No 1 (Hudswell Clarke, built 1865), No 4 (Black Hawthorn, of 1866), No 6 (Coulthard, of 1864) and No 20 (Stephenson of 1876), some of these with outside frames, there were locomotives built at Lambton Engine Works and several from South Wales railways. The Taff Vale was represented by three 0-6-0Ts, NCB Nos 52/3/4, formerly GWR Nos 426/48/75, of classes 'O2', 'O' and 'O1' respectively, and two ex-Cardiff Railway 0-6-2Ts, formerly GWR Nos 156/59.

The following year, 1954, found us in camping apartments at Culross, Fife. The station was right on the edge of the Firth of Forth, looking across to the

Left: Period piece: a GWR camping coach, as photographed in July 1934. *BR*

Right: An LNER exhibition at Romford in June 1936, with Stratford 'Coffee-pot' 0-4-0ST attached to an ex-Manchester, Sheffield and Lincolnshire Rly coach, converted to a camping coach. *E. R. Wethersett/Ian Allan Library*

ports of Bo'ness and Grangemouth and with a distant view of the Forth Bridge. Cooking and lighting here were by gas. The passenger service on this branch had been withdrawn, but there was a good bus service to Dunfermline. The two other closed stations between Culross and Dunfermline, Torryburn and Cairneyhill, had also been adapted as camping apartments.

We took out holiday runabout tickets, and journeys from Dunfermline enabled us to visit the Alva branch, closed to passengers at the end of October that year, the Methil branch, on which our train was drawn by 'C15' 4-4-2T No 67452 (ex-NBR No 1), and Dundee.

Visits of railway interest were made to St Margaret's, Polmont and Dawsholm sheds, and to the Bo'ness branch. At Coltness Ironworks we photographed their No 11, a former Barry Railway 0-6-0ST, still largely in original condition. This engine, formerly BR No 49 and later GWR No 712, was conveniently shunting outside the office buildings.

In 1955 our initial applications were unsuccessful but we accepted a cancelled booking for one week at the Kettleness coach on the Whitby-Middlesbrough coast line. This, our first camping coach, was an ex-GER vehicle, and when there was a strong wind, it swayed quite noticeably. At the next station, Sandsend, there were as many as six coaches quite close to the beach, but the Kettleness coach was located on a cliff high above the sea. Oil was in use here for cooking and lighting. There were useful runabout tickets from Staithes to Scarborough at a cost of only 10/- (50p) for the week enabling us to visit both those two places as well as Whitby and Robin's Hood Bay. We also went to Goathland, much more widely known today because of its location on the North Yorkshire Moors Railway.

Locomotives noted working on the coast line through Kettleness during our stay were very varied and included examples of each of the ex-NER 'J25' and 'J26' 0-6-0 classes; a 'Q6' 0-8-0; a 'G5' 0-4-4T; several 'A8' 4-6-2Ts; LNER 'B1s'; 'A5' 4-6-2Ts; a 'V1' and 'V3' 2-6-2Ts; various LMS and BR Standard 2-6-0s and BR Standard 2-6-4Ts

Seaham Harbour was visited and the Company's engine *Mars* was seen at work. This 0-6-0ST was a former NER engine numbered 1661 in the NER list before its sale in 1908. She was of the early and once popular long-boiler type with all the wheels ahead of the firebox. Lambton Engine Works was again an

object of attention as it had been two years earlier. The third call that day was to Backworth Collieries. Seen here were an 0-6-0PT, ex-GWR No 714, originally a Barry Railway saddle tank, and an ex-Port Talbot Railway 0-6-0ST which became GWR No 813 and is now preserved on the Severn Valley Railway. Other interesting engines here were three 0-6-0STs bearing NCB Nos 1/3/4, formerly NER Nos 1357, 1775/797 respectively. No 4 was another of the long-boiler type earlier referred to, but No 3, which had just been condemned, had been rebuilt about 1915 with trailing wheels behind the firebox.

During our holiday that year it was unusual to see two derailments in three days. Class 'J25' No 65656 was derailed at points in Kettleness goods yard, while on the journey home we were in York station when Class 'A4' No 60026 *Miles Beevor* had apparently started on receiving the platform right-away, but passed the departure signal at red and ended up with all the engine wheels off the line at the first set of points.

The north-east of England was again our destination in 1956, this time being Middleton-in-Teesdale camping cottage. On this well-kept station with its flower beds and hanging baskets, we had electricity for cooking and lighting. We used the train service to Barnard Castle and with holiday runabout tickets visited Darlington, Middlesbrough, Richmond, Whitby and other places on the coast. Opposite our cottage was the stone-built shed for the branch locomotive, and at 05.30 every day while still abed, we could hear a 'G5' 0-4-4T (either No 67284 or 305) emerge to work the first departure at 06.23. The first arrival at the station was at 07.30, often hauled by 'A8' 4-6-2T No 69875; the return journey of this train was the well-filled 07.40, whose departure was usually the signal for us to get up.

That year we had something of a rail tour by way of Darlington and Newcastle to Carlisle, where a call was made at Canal sheds. We also journeyed up the Waverley route as far as Hawick, enabling the shed there to be visited. Former NBR locomotives seen on this section were of LNER classes 'J35', 'J36', 'N15', 'C16' and 'D30'. Six of the 'D30' 'Scott' class 4-4-0 also were noted. The journey home from Hawick was via Riccarton and Hexham by the attractive Border Counties Railway, the NBR-owned line which penetrated far into England, then back to Newcastle and so home via Darlington.

Other railway trips took us to Broomhill Colliery, near Amble, where an 0-6-0T, formerly Llanelly & Mynydd Mawr Railway *George Waddell* still carried her GWR numberplate 312. At North and South Blyth sheds, all but one of the thirty-two locomotives seen were of NER origin, comprising 0-6-0s of Classes 'J25' and 'J27', 0-6-0Ts of Class 'J77' and 0-4-4Ts of

Far left: Ex-NER Fletcher outside-framed 0-6-0 No 658, as NCB No 3, at Seaton Delaval in September 1953. *Author*

Railway camping accommodation on terra firma. *Right:* Camping cottage at Middleton-in-Teesdale. *Below right:* Camping apartments at Kilmany. *Both: Author*

Class 'G5'. One special memory is of the 'J77' tanks storming up to the staithes with loaded coal wagons.

For the 1957 and 1958 summers we booked at Kilmany on the NBR North of Fife line, which had lost its passenger service in 1951. Many chairs on the track were lettered N&NFR (Newburgh and North Fife Railway). The camping apartments here were kept in first-class condition by porter-in-charge, Robert Brown, and his efforts had earned a thick file of appreciative letters from campers. Once again paraffin was used for cooking and lighting. An infrequent bus service connected with the trains from St Fort station to Dundee. Runabout tickets on both holidays took us to Carnoustie, Arbroath, Montrose, Perth, Crieff, Comrie, Aberfeldy, Balquhidder and Callander. One day we paid excess fares beyond the limits of our 'runabouts' to cross Druimuachdar Summit and reach Dalwhinnie in Inverness-shire. We felt quite adventurous so far from our holiday home on such tenuous connections, dependent on good timekeeping by the trains to connect with the last bus home.

St Fort station had only a sparse return service in the evening, but in the morning we could book a single to Wormit, the first station south of the Tay Bridge on the Dundee-Tayport branch. An interesting thing about this ticket was that although three stations only were covered, the short journey involved crossing the Tay Bridge twice on a single ticket. We broke our journey at Dundee in the morning, returning thence in the evening to Wormit with its more frequent train service and so home by bus.

One treat for railway campers was a ride on the local goods to shunt at Luthrie and Lindores further along the branch. Our trip was with NBR 'J37' 0-6-0 No 64598 which left Kilmany for Lindores with two campers on the footplate and the rest of the party in the guard's van. The stop made at a farm crossing to pick up a box of eggs is unlikely to have been shown in the working timetable! The return journey, tender-first into driving rain, was a reminder of one of the less glamorous experiences met with by footplate men.

From Kilmany visits could be conveniently made to sheds in the Edinburgh and Glasgow areas. Steam was still plentiful, with a good selection of ex-CR and ex-NBR types to be seen. LMS and LNER Pacifics were also hard at work, together with various BR classes. Near Glasgow we saw Gartsherrie Iron

Works' ex-GER 'J15' 0-6-0, formerly LNER No 7690, resplendent with polished brass dome, red coupling rods and lined black livery. Greenock, reputed to be the wettest place in Scotland, certainly lived up to its reputation on our visit. There Pickersgill 4-4-0s Nos 54468/79/98 represented the CR at Princes Pier shed while a footplate trip on 2-6-4T No 42264 over the two miles from Ladyburn shed to Greenock West, the nearest point to Princes Pier shed, was not only a welcome surprise but also a means of avoiding the rain. Return to Glasgow was made from Princes Pier station by the G&SWR route, now curtailed at Kilmacolm.

In the case of both the holidays at Kilmany the journeys home to Cheshire took us between Edinburgh and Carlisle by the scenic Waverley Route. In the Hawick area some of the dwindling stock of NBR 'Scotts' and 'Glens' were seen. In June 1958 there was an exhibition at Carlisle Citadel station to mark the 8th centenary of the granting of the city's charter. The historic engines on display were not so readily seen then as now and comprised MR 4-2-2 No 118, CR 4-2-2 No 123, FR 0-4-0 No 3, LNWR 2-4-0 *Hardwicke* and 2-2-2 *Cornwall*, together with some historic carriages.

For 1959 and 1961 our holidays were in a camping coach at Tyndrum Lower station in Western Perthshire. Stabled in the goods yard below the former CR station on the Oban line, this coach was at probably the most picturesque of any of our railway locations. Encircled by mountains and well away from the main road our coach and its surroundings would have made a fine holiday even without moving from the immediate district. One lasting memory is that of travelling from Tyndrum by the 07.27 Glasgow train through Strath Fillan and Glen Dochart towards Glenoglehead summit. After two days of continuous rain the bright morning sunshine brought out the colours of the surrounding countryside and mountains giving passengers some of the finest views in Scotland. Half a mile away, on the other side of the strath, on the Fort William line is the ex-NBR Tyndrum Upper station, which boasted a camping coach before the last war. So steep is the approach to this station that the roadway to it climbs by a wide zig-zag course, although there is access on foot by way of a footpath straight up the mountain-side.

There was railway interest at night, too. Goods trains toiled up the strath in the dark, but the echoing of their exhausts made it difficult to decide which of the two lines was being used on the approach to Tyndrum. Sometimes, the puzzle was solved when the sudden glare across the strath from an opened firebox door indicated a train climbing on the more-distant West Highland Line.

Our own station had some notable features. Being 770ft above sea-level the rail approach from the south was so steep that most down stopping trains steamed right up to the far end of the platform. Out of sight of passing trains, our coach was at a lower level in the goods yard, an area which included the site of the original station built there in 1873, when for four years

lack of funds deferred continuation of the line towards Oban. On one occasion a tablet failure meant nearly an hour's wait at Tyndrum for an Oban-bound train. Passengers, driver and fireman left the train and climbed the mountain-side above the station, gathering heather until recalled in good time by the guard's whistle.

We had chosen Tyndrum for our holiday partly because trains were available from this tiny village in four directions: to Oban and Ballachulish through the Pass of Brander, to Fort William over Rannoch Moor, to Callander and Stirling and to Loch Lomond through Glen Douglas. As usual we booked holiday runabout tickets, visiting all the places mentioned, together with the Killin branch. We paid excess fares to reach Mallaig, had a steamer trip on Loch Lomond and even crossed Rannoch Moor from Glencoe by one of the few bus services provided. Those days most railway routes enjoyed more frequent services than they do today, and, of course, the Callander line is no more. In the evening it was pleasant to leave the train at Tyndrum, in the heart of the Highlands, to enjoy the comfort of our coach in its glorious surroundings, when most of the other passengers were bound for the busy cities of Glasgow and Edinburgh or for places farther south. Apart from a general store in Tyndrum village the nearest group of shops was 24 miles away at Killin, although a butcher there would, if phoned, put meat on the train to reach us by mid-morning.

There was much of interest in our ordinary train journeys, but special trips were made to visit Ardrossan, Polmadie and Bathgate sheds, the last-named containing many stored NBR engines. A memorable sight on the Polmadie visit in 1959 was that of the unexpected appearance of one of the special trains run to Glasgow for the Scottish Industries Exhibition. Passing by in two shades of sparkling green came two preserved 4-4-0 engines, the GNSR *Gordon Highlander* leading the GWR's *City of Truro*. On the 1961 holiday we travelled over the Lanark to Muirkirk line, and also visited Hurlford, Ayr and Dawsholm sheds. At the last of these were four of the engines now preserved in the Glasgow Transport Museum: CR Single No 123, GNSR 4-4-0 No 49, HR 4-6-0 No 103 and NBR 'Glen' No 256, while HR No 54398 *Ben Alder* was rusting in the open, awaiting an unwarranted fate.

In 1960 we made an unsuccessful application for a

Above left: An ex-LSWR restaurant car, as Southern Railway camping coach No 25, at Hinton Admiral in June 1948. *J. H. Aston*

Contrasts in camping coaches. *Left:* Ex-CR coach at Tyndrum Lower. *Right:* The dining room of an LMR-allocated Pullman vehicle, at Bettws-y-Coed. *Author; BR*

camping coach at Combpyne on the interesting Lyme Regis branch, and in place accepted a cancellation for one of four coaches at a station in South Devon, the only occasion in our railway camping holidays when there was more than one coach at out location. Our accommodation was in an ex-SECR carriage, slightly narrower than the coaches we had previously stayed in, and it was surprising how the missing inches were noticed. The carriage had suffered some rough handling from former tenants and had a neglected look. We also had the unfortunate experience of having the bedding replaced and the coach fumigated; every other coach we used was quite beyond reproach. The weather was unsettled with little sunshine, so that this holiday was the least enjoyable of any. With runabout tickets we visited places of interest in North and South Devon, and crossed into East Cornwall twice.

Two rail trips were outstanding, the first being to Wadebridge to see the LSWR Beattie 2-4-0WTs. Their popularity was indicated by the large number of shed-pass advices in the foreman's office. With thunder and lightning overhead Beattie No 30586 shunted in the goods yard, while 30587 came through the station, bunker-first, on a china-clay train from Wenford Bridge. The third engine, No 30585, was at Eastleigh Works at the time. The second occasion was a journey on the Lyme Regis branch, where LSWR Adams 4-4-2T No 30583 was on passenger duty on this steeply-graded and sharply-curved line.

The Western Region were our hosts for the first time in 1962, and we had a roomy eight-berth GWR coach at Llanrhystyd Road, the first station out of Aberystwyth on the old Manchester & Milford Railway. The coach was in a siding a short distance from the station, involving a longer walk than usual for water supplies. For the coach at the next station, Llanilar, however, water had to be delivered daily by train.

With tickets covering the Cambrian Coast line we visited many of the coastal resorts, railway interest journeys took in trips on the Vale of Rheidol and Talyllyn lines, and we also visited Kidwelly to see the now-preserved 0-6-0ST *Margaret*, formerly belonging to the Gwendraeth Valleys Railway and originally built in 1878 for the North Pembrokeshire & Fishguard Railway. This engine was in a shed at the former tinplate works and was quite isolated from any rail access. Moving on to Neath the day's outing was continued over the moors by the Neath & Brecon Railway to Brecon, then by way of the picturesque Mid-Wales line of the former Cambrian Railways to Moat Lane Junction, and from there we continued to Aberystwyth. By the end of 1962 such a round trip could no longer be made in view of the withdrawal of passenger services from the lines between Neath, Brecon and Moat Lane Junction.

The next year we were again on the Western Region, our fortnight being spent at the Cheddar

camping coach. The station had a fine all-over roof of Bristol & Exeter Railway origin, and there were still GWR engines at work on the branch, including '22xx' 0-6-0s, '57xx' 0-6-0PTs and a '4575' 2-6-2T. The volume of passenger traffic was very small indeed, and the service was withdrawn later the same year. Our holiday coincided with the strawberry-picking season, and much of the fruit was sent away by special van trains to London and elsewhere. Runabout tickets from Yatton, where the branch joined the main line, gave access to interesting places in Somerset, and we travelled over the Somerset and Dorset line.

In 1964 we stayed at Akeld station in Northumberland, on the branch line from Wooler to Coldstream, where the converted premises were the roomiest we encountered. Calor gas was used for cooking, and we had oil lamps. The platform area in front of the rooms was enclosed with glazed partitions, and there was a glass verandah overhead, so that our rooms were light and airy. The station, we were told, had been built on a bog, and we were shown where in one place the platform had sunk.

We had an interesting trip in the brake van of the local goods train, hauled by 2-6-0 No 78024, for the $7\frac{1}{4}$ miles from Akeld to Mindrum. Steam locomotives were greatly reduced in numbers, but a visit to Percy Main shed found eleven engines, all ex-NER 'J27' 0-6-0s. In Scotland journeys were made over the branch lines to Kirkintilloch, Coalburn, Musselburgh and Corstorphine, shortly before their closure to passengers, while it was also possible to visit the Riverside branch from Newcastle upon Tyne and the short Alnwick branch with its fine array of North Eastern Railway signals, some of them of the old slotted-post type.

It was interesting to be able to inspect the traffic records from the date of the opening of Akeld station, on 5 September 1887, and these revealed that the number of passengers booked back in 1889 was maintained at broadly the same level up to 1920. From then a steady decline in numbers set in until closure to passengers came in September 1930. The years 1941-43 showed returns for passengers; presumably this was military traffic. Business in freight and parcels increased steadily up to 1920, but, afterwards, this also declined, although as late as 1950 traffic in fish and rabbits alone amounted to 66 tons.

Finally, we come to 1965, the last time we had a holiday with British Railways. The end was now in sight for railway camping holidays. No cottages or apartments were available from 1965 onwards, while camping coaches were also withdrawn on the North Eastern and Western Regions. However, we were able to get a booking at Inverkip on the Clyde Coast. This was the only time we had a Pullman coach and the inside was roomy. The lower parts of the finely-panelled wood inside the coach were covered with plywood to protect against damage. Wooden blocks had been fixed to the bogie springs to steady the coach in windy weather. Calor gas was provided for cooking and lighting.

Inverkip station was beautifully kept under the station-master, Mr Law; hanging baskets decorated the platforms, and shrubs were planted between the running lines. We visited places on the Clyde coast and went north to Loch Lomond and The Trossachs.

Inverkip station was busy from the first freight at about 06.00 to the last train at about 20.30. Soon to be electrified, duties on the line were shared by steam and diesel traction. Two special train trips were made, one of these being to Stranraer, the Dumfries to Stranraer route having been closed to all traffic only the previous month. The other journey was to visit the GNSR Deeside line, which by then was under threat of closure. Some LNER Pacifics were still at work, 'A4s' Nos 60006/24/31 being noted between Glasgow and Aberdeen.

So ended thirteen consecutive and enjoyable annual holidays as paying guests of British Railways. By 1965 the number of camping coaches had gradually diminished, and one can only suggest various causes which may have led to their decline. The closure of so many branch lines to all traffic, the withdrawal of all staff from many smaller stations, especially in suitable holiday areas, and the growing popularity of motoring holidays were all contributory. Eventually British Railways decided that the thirty remaining camping coaches on the seven different sites at Abergele, Blackpool, Seascale and on the Cambrian Coast should not be offered from 1972 onwards. Camping coaches had of course a special appeal for railway enthusiasts in providing a holiday with close and frequent contact with railways from the lineside, but coaches were, of course, occupied for other purposes. Family holidays with children gave one a freedom not so easily found elsewhere. One site had been booked by a group of nurses who had trained together, and who came together again for a reunion holiday.

Before World War 2 the LNER experimented with a touring coach, which was taken by train each day to a different site in the Yorkshire Dales and Moors. There was also the luxurious 'Northern Belle' cruise train on which passengers lived for a week, leaving Kings Cross to visit attractive places in North-East England and on the LNER lines in Scotland.

Along with the passing of many other once-familiar features of our railways, the end of camping coaches marked the close of an era. But, for many of those who occupied the sites there remain memories of experiences, varied, unexpected or just peaceful and happy, provided by a unique type of holiday no longer available on British Rail.

The versatile Class 31s

The Class 31s, built by Brush Electrical Engineering Co, of Loughborough, first entered BR service in the autumn of 1957. Eighty or so had been completed before they were allocated outside East Anglia, but they then became a feature of the southern end of the East Coast main line, and in the Sheffield area. By the late 1960s they were beginning to be transferred further afield and now, nearly 25 years since the earliest examples, the Class 31/0s, started work, the Class 31s are widely spread geographically and used on all sorts of trains, as this photo-feature shows.

Below: In the late 1970s, consistent passenger workings for WR-based Class 31s were found on the Bristol-Portsmouth trains. On 24 May 1977, not long after loco-hauled stock replaced dmus on these services, 31.293 is seen between Bradford Junctions and Trowbridge on the 17.12 Bristol-Portsmouth Harbour. *G. R. Hounsell*

Left: Photographs of bullion trains are few and far between. 'Custom'-liveried 31.411 powers one such working near Rossington, on the East Coast main line, on 8 September 1978. *S. J. Turner*

Below: Holidaymakers in the rain (1): 31.168 leaves Bridlington with a Scarborough-Hull train on a wet August Saturday afternoon in August 1978. *D. A. Flitcroft*

Bottom: Holidaymakers in the rain (2): Dawlish is suffering a torrential rainstorm on 25 August 1979, as 31.259/213 bring a Saturday holiday train, the 14.25 Paignton-Oxford, into the station. *Mark S. Wilkins*

Right: The Class 31s have had a long association with the GE Cambridge line. A murky December day in 1978 finds 31.112 arriving at Cambridge on a Liverpool St-Kings Lynn train. *Michael Rhodes*

Centre right: Typical of the variety of freight work undertaken by the Class 31s. No 31.155 shunts grain hoppers at a private siding at Gainsborough in July 1977. *Stanley Creer*

Bottom right: The sad remains of the abandoned Seaton Junction station are passed by the 19.55 Exeter St Davids-Basingstoke in the charge of an unidentified '31' in July 1977. *Brian Morrison*

The era of the
diesel prototype

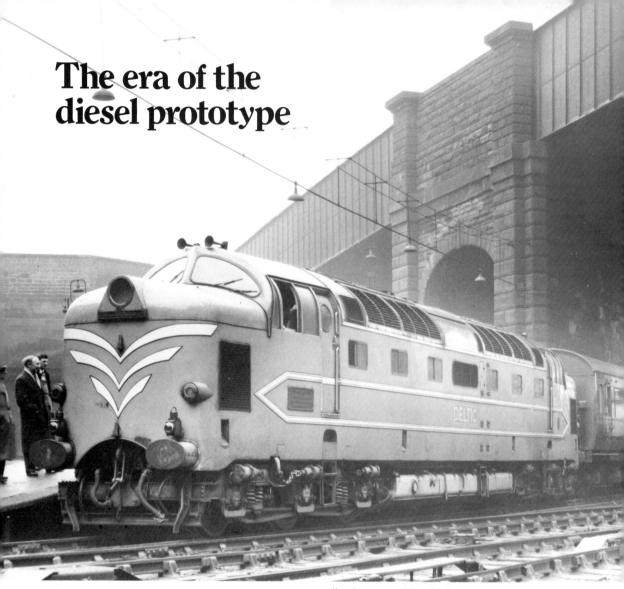

STEPHEN J. CHAPMAN

What have birds of prey, big cats and a letter from the Greek alphabet, got in common? They all gave names to locomotives of the diesel prototype era which lasted broadly from 1955 to 1971.

With plenty of cheap coal available, the railway companies, and British Railways in its first few years, were content to perpetuate steam designs for main line work rather than invest in a new diesel fleet or in large scale electrification. Apart from shunting locomotives, only half a dozen or so main line diesels had been brought into service before the announcement of the British Railways' 1955 Modernisation Plan. The Plan envisaged the total replacement of steam by electric or

diesel power within 20-25 years and, although steam locomotives continued to be built up to 1960, by 1958 main line diesel locomotives were being introduced at an increasing rate.

The Modernisation Plan provided a new impetus to the private sector of the British locomotive industry, hitherto struggling to interest BR in dieselisation and, until then, relying on orders from overseas railways and industrial users.

English Electric was the first of the British locomotive manufacturers to produce a prototype main line diesel for trials on the BR, a locomotive which proved immensely successful leading to a production series which became the backbone of the East Coast main line Inter-City motive power fleet.

The Company had been searching for some time for

Left: A late 1950s' picture of the prototype *Deltic* leaving Liverpool Lime St station on an express for London. *GEC Traction*

line, showing itself to be more than capable on the heavy Liverpool and Perth turns to and from Euston. Following intermediate overhaul, it was transferred to service trials on the East Coast main line, proving a great success. The relatively straight alignment and favourable gradients of the East Coast route meant that high speeds could be sustained, allowing *Deltic* to show its paces.

The London Midland Region was already committed to 25kV ac electrification for the West Coast route and so showed no interest in the potential of *Deltic*. On the East Coast route, despite a price-tag of £250,000 for each locomotive, the production 'Deltics' proved to be a sound investment as the 22 of the class were available to do the jobs of no less than 55 Pacifics.

The *Deltic* prototype was not without problems. Its size brought loading gauge difficulties and a top speed of 90mile/h, although ideal for the requirements of the 1950s, had to be raised to meet the 100mile/h maxima which railway management sought for the principal express passenger trains of the 1960s. The production 'Deltics' first appeared early in 1961 with a number of detailed modifications compared with the prototype. The overall length of the locomotive was reduced from 69ft 6in to 67ft 9in, and a slightly reduced body profile eliminated the loading gauge problems. The Type '5s' — as they were designated — were also lighter, weighing only 99 tons compared with the 106 tons of the prototype; in each case the power/weight ratio was particularly good. To meet the operating requirements of the next decade and beyond, the top speed was increased to 100mile/h and the fuel capacity raised from 800 to 900 gallons.

A major difference between prototype and production units lay in the generator and traction motors. The prototype was equipped with a generator running at 1,500rev/min but the Type '5s' had generators of 1,125rev/min rating, the crankshaft speed from the engine being reduced by the output gearing. Also the production series was equipped with four-pole traction motors, whereas the prototype had a six-pole type.

Externally, the body superstructure was somewhat smoothed to reduce wind resistance; gone was the distinctive headlamp on the top of the nose, instead there was a four-character headcode indicator at each end, and, in place of the prototype's blue livery, an attractive two-tone green livery.

As the first production 'Deltics' were about to enter service, the prototype was withdrawn, having run some 400,000 miles in six years. English Electric restored *Deltic* to pristine condition at Vulcan Foundry and presented her to the Science Museum,

a land application for the Napier Deltic diesel engine which had been a great success when used in Naval patrol boats. The outcome of its efforts came in 1955 when the prototype *Deltic* Co-Co emerged from EE's Preston Works, powered by two of the Napier two-stroke D18-25 engines from which the prototype took its name. Each engine generated 1,650hp at 1,500rev/min, providing a total of 3,300hp — considered quite remarkable even today, let alone in 1955, and making the *Deltic* the most powerful single locomotive in the world at that time, and for some while after. *Deltic* was finished in blue livery with three pale yellow whiskers, or chevrons, on the nose at each end and the Deltic legend on each side between two pale yellow bands.

Deltic went into service on the West Coast main

Above: Deltic on the East Coast main line and about to cross the River Idle, near Ordsall, Retford, with the 08.20 Kings Cross-Doncaster on 28 February 1959.   *K. R. Pirt*

Left: The combination of the prototype *Deltic* hauled by Class 37 No D6822 makes an unusual sight at Rugby Midland on 24 April 1963, during the course of *Deltic's* trip to the Science Museum for preservation.   *John F. Hughes*

The two EE 500hp prototype shunters. *Below left:* D0226, as preserved on the Keighley and Worth Valley Railway, and seen in 1969. *Below:* The elusive D227, at Stratford, ER, in May 1959.   *C. P. Boocock; R. A. Panting*

Right: The prototype *Taurus* 600hp 0-8-0, built by Yorkshire Engine Co Ltd.

London, where she now stands as a proud monument to a major step forward in the development of diesel rail traction.

When *Deltic* was still undergoing trials, English Electric produced two prototype 0-6-0 diesel locomotives in 1957 intended for heavy shunting and trip working. The Company had already sewn-up the market for the standard 350hp diesel electric shunter, and BR was in the middle of constructing over 1,000 examples to this design. But EE considered that there might be a market for a 500hp design with a top speed of 40mile/h for a wider range of duties.

Of the two locomotives originally numbered D226 and D227, the first was equipped with electric transmission and the latter with hydraulic transmission in order to assess the relative merits of each type. In 1959 the pair were renumbered D0226 and D0227 to avoid confusion with the BR 2,000hp Type '4s' being constructed by English Electric at the time.

Both the shunters featured English Electric's type 6RKT 750rev/min diesel engines. For power to wheels No D0226 had one English Electric traction motor driving in the same manner as the 350hp shunters and D0227 had a Lysholm-Smith torque converter and direct drive to the axles. No D0226 began its trials at Speke Junction shed, Liverpool, working freight and coaching stock turns in the Edge Hill area and into Lime Street. In 1959 it was transferred to the Eastern Region, working at Doncaster, Sheffield and Stratford, before moving to Bristol where it took up local freight, and some coaching stock turns around Bristol and Chippenham. The movements of D0227 do not appear to have been so well-documented and it would be interesting to know more about them.

In 1960 English Electric returned both locomotives to their works, D0226 to Vulcan Foundry and D0227 is thought to have gone to Preston. There they remained either in store or were used as works shunters for the rest of their time. D0227 was cut up some time later but, in 1966, D0226 was presented to the Keighley and Worth Valley Light Railway, where it can be seen today. By the late 1970s, as part of the GEC group, the former Vulcan Foundry was turning out similarly powered diesel electric and diesel hydraulic shunters for UK and overseas markets.

The Yorkshire Engine Company, of Meadow Hall Works, Sheffield, also made a bid for the higher rated shunter market by producing a prototype 0-8-0 centre cab diesel-hydraulic named *Taurus* in 1961. Well-known as a manufacturer of industrial locomotives, by this time the Company was struggling to stay in business and hoping to improve its prospects by plugging the gap between the 350hp shunters and the Type '1' Bo-Bos on BR, or failing that, to win further industrial orders, particularly for heavy-duty steelworks duties.

Taurus was a direct descendant of the BR Fell 2-D-2 diesel mechanical locomotive of 1951, No 10100, having a unique feature by which only one, or both, of its two Rolls-Royce C8SFL vertical eight-cylinder engines might be used at any one time. Of the torque converters, also of Rolls-Royce manufacture, one was driven through a Hardy-Spicer cardan shaft and the other through a set of 1:875 to 1 spur gears. Both were brought together on the driving axle by a system of bevel gears. With only one engine running *Taurus* developed 310hp at 1,800rev/min, giving a top speed of 12mile/h. The second engine could be engaged at any speed above 3½mile/h, without causing a break in torque or tractive effort. With both engines operating, a total output of 720hp was achieved and a top speed of 36mile/h could be maintained.

The prototype 0-8-0 saw service on BR in the Sheffield area in 1961 but was soon transferred to the Western Region, being based at St Philip's Marsh shed, Bristol, where it worked until October of the same year and then began trials on the Eastern Region at Stratford.

Although no order was forthcoming from BR, Yorkshire Engine Co was successful in its attempts to market the *Taurus* design to industry. Orders were received for 0-6-0 versions as well as the 0-8-0 type and a number were delivered to the steel industry before the Yorkshire Engine Co finally ceased business. In the meantime some had been sold to overseas users.

In 1961 Brush Electrical Engineering of Loughborough sought to break English Electric's apparently firm grip on BR's Type '4' diesel electric main line locomotive requirements by producing a powerful diesel electric prototype, the *Falcon*. Weighing in at 115 tons, *Falcon* was equipped with Maybach type MD655 twelve-cylinder vee engines, offering a total output of 2,800hp. Apart from the 'Deltics', the locomotive was the only main line diesel electric in Britain of Type '4' classification or over with fast-running engines. The Maybachs operated at 1,500rev/min. Naturally enough, Brush was responsible for all the electrical equipment, including six four-pole axle-hung traction motors. One other

distinction was that *Falcon* had a maximum speed of 100mile/h.

Falcon, numbered D0280, began trials in October 1961 on the Western Region, and in a distinctive golden sand livery soon made its mark on the Bristol and West of England main lines. The following year *Falcon* was transferred to Finsbury Park and assigned to the 'Master Cutler' Pullman services between Kings Cross and Sheffield.

During 18 months of trials the Brush prototype completed no less than 120,000 miles and was aided, no doubt, by a 1,300 gallon fuel capacity. *Falcon* also pulled off some quite amazing feats of strength, such as restarting 638 tons of empty passenger stock on the 1 in 38 of the Lickey incline and 550 ton loads on 1 in 37 and 1 in 50 gradients on South Devon banks.

Although at the time BR did not pursue the idea of fast-running diesel engines for main line service, the performance of the Maybach engines was regarded as impressive, and the locomotive's general outline and mechanical parts design were adopted as standard for a new breed of Co-Co diesel electrics ordered from Brush by BR and delivered from 1962 onwards. These were, of course, later to be well-known as the Class 47s. In the same period, the Maybach type MD655 engines were going into service on BR, being installed in the 'Western' class diesel hydraulics being built at Swindon and Crewe Works.

As *Falcon's* engines were standard with those of the 'Western' class, it was logical enough that when the Eastern Region trials were completed in 1965, *Falcon* moved over to service on the Western Region, to aid maintenance, although Brush continued to be responsible for the care of the electrical equipment. At the same time the golden sand livery made way for a more or less standard BR two-tone green, although the

locomotive retained the number D0280 and the Falcon motif, the latter commemorating the locomotive's birthplace at Falcon Works, Loughborough. The two-tone green livery later gave way to BR standard blue and in 1971 *Falcon* was designated Class 53, being renumbered 1200. During BR operation it was allocated to Bristol Bath Rd, Cardiff Canton, and Ebbw Junction, Newport depots. No 1200 spent its latter days at Ebbw Junction hauling coal trains. Following this there was a period of storage at Derby when its withdrawal was rumoured. However, the locomotive returned to Newport to do at least another year's useful work before finally succumbing to the breaker's torch at Cashmore's Newport yard at the end of 1975.

Shortly after *Falcon's* introduction, a rival 100mile/h locomotive appeared on the scene, this being a promotion by a consortium of three companies, the Birmingham Railway Carriage and Wagon Co, Associated Electrical Industries and Sulzer. This locomotive, No D0260 *Lion* was officially 'launched' by BRCW's chairman, Mr F. D. O'Brian Newman at the Company's Smethwick Works on 25 May 1962.

Lion's external lines were somewhat similar to those of Brush's *Falcon*, but in many other ways it was revolutionary. Not only did it carry an attractive and probably unique white livery, lined out in black, but it sported reinforced plastic doors and a translucent roof trap of the same material which could be pneumatically raised to let the engine heat escape before carrying out maintenance work. Fitted with both steam and electric train heating equipment *Lion* made extensive use of rubber suspension components, such as Alsthom-type rubber cone pivots on the bogies. Its most significant feature was the single Sulzer 12LDA28C diesel engine rated at 2,750hp and

with an engine speed of 800rev/min, making *Lion* the most powerful single-engined diesel locomotive which had yet appeared in Britain. The twelve-cylinder 12LDA28C was a development of the 2,500hp LDA28B engine, already used for the BR-Sulzer 'Peak' class. AEI was responsible for all the electrical equipment including six Type 253 nose-suspended traction motors.

Extensive use of reinforced plastics for super-structure components contributed to keeping down weight and *Lion's* 114 tons was spread over a Co-Co wheel arrangement, giving an axle load of only 19 tons. Total length over buffers was 63ft 6in and the fuel capacity 850 gallons.

Lion's programme of trials was much the same as for *Falcon*, involving WR and ER main lines and, like her Brush-built contemporary, *Lion* was able to restart 638 tons on Lickey incline. She worked on the Western Region until September 1963 putting in frequent appearances on Birmingham line expresses and then moved to the East Coast main line, regularly working the 04.00 Kings Cross to Leeds and the up 'Yorkshire Pullman'.

Unfortunately, *Lion* did not find favour, either with BR or, for that matter, with foreign administrations, and in any case was pipped at the post by the Brush 2,750hp Class 47s, which similarly featured the

Below left: Falcon, about to restart a test train on the Lickey Incline. Ex-Western Region dynamometer car next the locomotive. *Brush*

Right: Lion at Birmingham RC&W Co Ltd; the body is being strain-gauged under a loaded condition.

Below: Lion at Shrewsbury in 1962, when working a Paddington-Birkenhead train, and contrasting with 'Castle' No 5031 *Totnes Castle*. *GEC Traction*

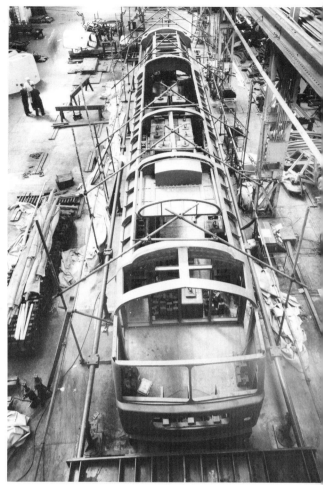

Sulzer 12LDA28C engine. Also, by the end of 1963 BRCW was in financial trouble and it was clear that *Lion* could not be sustained on trial by the remaining two companies. It was hoped that the locomotive might be added to BR's capital stock but as she possessed non-standard components this was not practicable and on returning to BRCW's Smethwick Works at the end of 1963 her fate was to be dismantled. The Sulzer engine was returned to its manufacturers Vickers, at Barrow, where it was completely reconditioned and, having run a relatively low mileage, was then installed in a new Class 47. All the electrical equipment was returned to AEI Trafford Park, Manchester and the other components sold. *Lion's* empty shell them made its sad final journey to Thomas Ward's Sheffield scrapyard where it was cut up.

English Electric returned to the prototype scene in May 1962 with its DP2, with what was to prove

Above: DP2 approaches Warrington with a Euston-Perth express on 5 October 1962. *J. R. Carter*

Below: In 'Deltic' type livery, DP2 nears Grantham with the down 'Flying Scotsman' on 27 March 1967; this was a regular turn for DP2 at the time. *J. H. Cooper-Smith*

another highly successful experimental diesel electric locomotive. The power unit used the updated, charge air-cooled version of the 16SVT engine which was already giving sterling service in the 2,000hp Type 4 1-Co-Co-1s introduced from 1958.

DP2, which was built at Vulcan Foundry, was almost identical in appearance to the production 'Deltics' but there the likeness ended, for naturally enough her internal layout was very different. The 16 CSVT was a medium speed engine running at 850rev/min and producing 2,700hp. However, the traction motors were the EE538A four-pole axle-hung type as used in the 'Deltics' and Type '3s'. Weighing 105 tons and 69ft 6in in length over the buffers, DP2 had a 900 gallon fuel tank and a top speed of 90mile/h.

At first, DP2 began trials on the West Coast main line, being based at Camden, and worked Euston-Carlisle, Crewe-Birmingham and Chester turns; the 07.45 Euston-Liverpool Lime St in particular became a regular assignment. During trials she was notching up 3,800-4,000 miles a week and, on 8 May 1962, shortly after entering service, took a 15-coach load of 475 tons past Tebay at 80mile/h.

In the summer of 1963, after completing some 164,000 miles on West Coast duties, DP2 was transferred to the Eastern Region at Finsbury Park and began work on the East Coast main line, frequently covering the 10.10 Kings Cross to Edinburgh and 22.30 return, Sheffield Pullmans and different diagrams at weekends. That September she became due for full overhaul, after completing 200,000 miles in service, and was sent to the former Robert Stephenson & Hawthorns works at Darlington, by now under EE ownership, where she was fitted with new bogies of a modified pattern which were currently being fitted to EE Type '3s' used on the Western Region for high-speed running. Following this, she ran for 58 consecutive days and 43,000 miles, without giving any cause for complaint. Another major overhaul followed in mid-1965, the locomotive having covered 360,000 miles in revenue earning service since 1962.

Proving a truly remarkable prototype, DP2 came just at the time when BR was looking for a high-speed diesel locomotive type to bridge the gap between steam and electrification on the West Coast main line north of Crewe. All were convinced this was the design they were looking for. DP2 had certainly proved herself on the gruelling climb to Shap and the EE electronic wheelslip protection, which in 1962 had enabled the locomotive to restart a 16-coach test train from Scout Green and attain 30mile/h within a few hundred yards, seemed an impressive and added bonus, ideal for this heavily graded route.

In time, a production version of this inspiring prototype was evolved but with very different equip-

Above: DP2 makes a sad sight at it is towed past Spen Jn, towards Huddersfield, en route to Vulcan Foundry on 8 September 1967. *B. J. Ashworth*

ment details, some comparatively untried, and 50 examples were built from 1967 onwards. One other unique aspect was that the 50 locomotives of Class 50, as they became known, were leased by BR from the manufacturers and remained the property of English Electric Leasing Ltd until purchased by BR only a few years ago.

Certainly the Class 50s were totally different in external appearance, having what in fact was considered as the standard BR cab, the more modern flat-front look giving them a very long appearance, despite being a foot shorter than the prototype. The 50s also came out a little heavier at 115 tons and had increased fuel capacity — up by around 150 gallons, useful for the long Crewe to Glasgow haul. Other features which were standard requirement for the late 1960s were a top speed of 100mile/h, electric train heating equipment, dual air/vacuum train braking and ability to operate in multiple — something that turned out vital for their operations on the West Coast route north of Crewe.

But just as the Class 50s were about to make their debut, DP2 met a tragic and untimely end at Thirsk on 31 July 1967. Some wagons of a northbound cement train travelling on the slow line of the four-track main line became derailed, fouling the fast line on which DP2 was travelling at speed with the 12.00 Kings Cross to Edinburgh, then a regular working for the locomotive. The express hit the derailed loaded wagons resulting in a bad accident in which seven lives were lost and DP2 was severely damaged. She was stored at York diesel depot for a short while before being towed back to Vulcan Foundry in September for an assessment of the repairs involved. As it turned out,

DP2 was so badly damaged that she was scrapped and so ended the career of what was probably the most successful of all the main line diesel locomotive prototypes, and one which had run no less than 600,000 miles with British Railways.

To date, the final prototype to come from the private sector appeared from Brush in January 1968, amid much publicity and press attention, with the distinction of being the most powerful single-engined diesel locomotive in the world. No HS (Hawker Siddeley) 4000 *Kestrel* was revolutionary, not only technically but also in appearance, having a streamlined body design and an eye-catching chocolate and yellow livery. *Kestrel* incorporated a French-built Sulzer sixteen-cylinder type LVA24 medium-speed engine which developed 4,000hp, and the Brush electrical equipment made much use of electronics. The locomotive's overall length was 66ft 6in.

Kestrel made a first public appearance in February 1968 at the head of a press demonstration train from Marylebone to Princes Risborough, after which it went for trials on the Eastern Region, first allocated to Shirebrook for freight train tests and then to Finsbury Park for East Coast main line duties.

In the light of widespread damage to the track on the West Coast main line, attributed to the Class 86 electrics and their axle-hung traction motors, BR decided to impose speed restrictions on some other locomotive classes which might be guilty of similar effects. *Kestrel* was considered to fall into this category and her maximum speed was therefore limited to 80mile/h. Her high axle loading of $21\frac{1}{2}$ tons was also thought to have contributed to a spate of certain types of rail failures on the East Coast main line. Although the locomotive did make its appearance on East Coast main line expresses, at a time when a future 'Deltic' replacement was being discussed, in the background plans were being laid for what later

became the High Speed Train and BR rapidly cooled to the *Kestrel*.

Kestrel was transferred back to Shirebrook depot for trials on merry-go-round coal trains but by this time it was clear that no orders were forthcoming from BR. It was withdrawn from these trials in 1971, and sold to the Soviet Union, having been rebogied for the 5ft gauge. The Russians had shown much interest in the locomotive's technology, and were known to be keen to develop a more modern series of high powered diesel locomotives. It is interesting to recall, in fact, that a Soviet trade delegation travelled on that first trip from Marylebone in 1968.

The sale of *Kestrel* in 1971 probably marked the end of an era which we are unlikely to witness again. The age of the diesel prototypes not only gave railway enthusiasts an alternative interest during the final days of steam, but provided the British railway industry and British Rail with the raw materials from which much of the current diesel traction fleet has been moulded.

My thanks are due to all those at British Rail, GEC Traction, Brush Electrical Machines and Sulzer for valuable assistance in the preparation of this article.

Above: Kestrel approaches Langley Jn with the 07.55 Kings Cross-Newcastle on 24 October 1969. *D. L. Percival*

Below: A probably unique view of *Kestrel* working on the Soviet Railways, after purchase in 1971; the headlight was fitted in the Soviet Union.

Over Aber water troughs comes Stanier '5' 4-6-0
No 44807 with down empty stock on
13 April 1966. *A. Wyn Hobson*

A look back at the North Wales coast main line

P. H. S. HAWORTH

For almost twelve years up until to August 1962 I lived at Penmaenmawr, Caernarvonshire, on the Chester-Holyhead main line. An interest in ships was replaced by trains in 1957, and this was when, at the age of eight, I began to compile my notes and lists. I clearly recall admiring the spotless 'Jubilee' No 45689 *Ajax* and Royal Scot' No 46127 *Old Contemptibles* at Bangor.

From September 1958, I attended a prep school at Bangor, and as my father taught English at another school there, we travelled together along the attractive coastal line ten miles from Penmaenmawr to Bangor every day. We caught the 08.17 from Penmaenmawr, a Llandudno Jn-Bangor train, and returned on the 16.20 from Bangor, each stopping at Aber and Llanfairfechan. This very acceptable routine was only varied by occasional journeys to Liverpool and Manchester and, more frequently, departures by the 09.54 to Chester for shopping expeditions. Latterly, I preceded my father's departure from Bangor by taking

55

the 15.52 for Crewe. This was a big step up, as this train did not call at Aber, and was hauled by a 'Jubilee' 4-6-0.

The Crewe train was usually brought from Holyhead by a 'Princess Coronation' Pacific, often in red livery, which stopped at the up end of Bangor's Platform 2 alongside the 'Jubilee' which would be waiting on the up fast line. The Pacific then drew forward to disappear briefly into the darkness of Bangor Tunnel, emerging with impressive calm on to the up relief line, before working a later departure. A mundane operation, perhaps, but it seemed to me to have a ceremonial air. The 'Jubilee' moved gently forward and then backed down on to the 15.52, and I was able to approve her lines at leisure before finding a compartment. 'Jubilees' appearing on this turn included Nos 45572 *Eire*, 45625 *Sarawak*, 45629 *Straits Settlements*, 45630 *Swaziland*, 45666 *Cornwallis*, 45684 *Jutland*, 45703 *Thunderer*, and best of all, the very clean 45600 *Bermuda* of Patricroft (26F).

During 1962 the train was often brought into Bangor by a Class 40 diesel-electric, to my sorrow, and I mourned the loss of the Stanier Pacific. There were several successive days of diesel haulage, and then, one Friday afternoon, I was delighted to see No 46256 *Sir William A. Stanier, FRS* burst into view at the mouth of Belmont Tunnel. She (or he) was succeeded by No 46257 *City of Salford*, the final member of the class.

The 16.20 for Llandudno Jn was virtually a school train and comprised five or six coaches hauled by an Ivatt '2' 2-6-2T, which ran bunker-first. Over a period of three years I noted Nos 41200/30/3/4/5/6/7/8/9 and 41322/3 on this duty; their performance was sprightly, and the acceleration from stops was swift. My father and I used to stand on the footbridge at Penmaenmawr and watch the train pull briskly out on its way to Conway. Many of the boys left the 16.20 at Llanfairfechan, but few used Aber. A girl-friend of mine lived there, and on alighting, a flight of portable wooden steps was provided for her access to the low platform. The station closed on 11 September, 1960.

Let's new relive a trip to Bangor on the 08.17 from Penmaenmawr in 1959. Arriving at the station, an austere Chester and Holyhead building, the down signals are pulled off well before the 08.17 is due. A BR Standard Caprotti valve gear Class '5', No 73127, advances rapidly down the long straight, past the gas-works and Pen-y-Cae, with express cattle vans for Holyhead. When the roar and clatter of the passing vans has died down, the up signals will be cleared, heralding the approach of the 07.30 Holyhead-Euston express. Here she is now at the overbridge, with 'Princess Coronation' Pacific No 46250 *City of Lichfield* rocking and swaying, as she leans to the

curve with fourteen or fifteen coaches, including a dining-car whose patrons breakfast imperturbably at 65mile/h. There's a rythmic pounding of steel on steel, a powerful draught and whirl of grit, twigs, leaves and papers, and then the red tail-light as the last van swings eastwards, followed by a rustle of signal-wires and restored calm. In sharp contrast, the 08.17 appears, slowing for the stop, with the scheduled 'Black Five' at its head. Today a 'mainstream' example is in charge — No 44802, one of the Derby-built series of 1944.

The simple designation '5MT 4-6-0' hid no fewer than eleven variations applied to those built 1947-51. The Class '5s' were all-pervading once the LMS Compounds had left North Wales and it needed a keen appreciation of the sequence of building of members of the class, and the deviations from the standard form, to compensate for the relative paucity of other locomotive classes seen. Trains on the North Wales coast could produce Caprotti '5's (Nos 44738/9/40/50) and the final twins of 1951 — Nos 44686/7. There were also the BR Standard '5s'.

The 08.17 generally consisted of five LMS coaches, as on this occasion, with a brake at each end, and often the guard's compartment in the leading vehicle was vacant. On this 1959 trip, I occupy the guard's seat directly beneath an end-window and watch No 44802 puffing purposefully up the 1 in 132 and into the deep cutting to Penmaenan. Penmaenmawr Tunnel, 453 yards long, is approached at each end through rock avalanche galleries whose apertures provide a novel alternation of light and shadow. The view opens towards Llanfairfechan, with the high hills of Snowdonia on the left, hills of many moods, flecked with snow even in April and May. The most imposing 'top' (of 3,091ft) of this range is Foel Fras, a lowering, form, dark against the sky, and visible from the train near Aber. On the right, across the saltings, Lavan Sands extend towards the Menai Straits and Anglesey. The sea is visible until the line passes beneath the A55 road at Llandegai.

A group of 16-ton all-steel mineral wagons usually stands in the down sidings at Llanfairfechan, a station built of local granite, and more attractive than Penmaenmawr. The up loop at Llanfairfechan (capacity 44 wagons) is normally unoccupied, but sometimes contains a long raft of Lowflats. Our '5', having passed Glanmor level crossing, takes water at Aber troughs, sousing the leading coach and distorting my view through the streaming pane. Pendredu level crossing precedes Aber station, which has a loop and sidings on the down side, and where business is light. The line ascends at 1 in 181 to Wig crossing, and continues to rise gently past Tairmeibion on a wooded embankment at 1 in 1527/227, where No 44802's white exhaust hangs momentarily in the wet air, shreds and disperses

Right: 'Jubilee' 4-6-0 No 45666 *Cornwallis* on an afternoon Bangor-Chester train near Bethesda Jn.   *J. D. Mills*

Below: 'Duchess' Pacific No 46231 *Duchess of Atholl* restarts the 09.20 Crewe-Holyhead from Bangor on 7 August 1961. *R. E. James-Robertson*

Bottom: Ivatt '2' 2-6-2T No 41233 moves empty stock out of Bangor in July 1964.   *E. N. Kneale*

among the trees as rabbits scutter out of sight. On the up side near this point, there is an isolated distant signal, with black and white banded tubular steel post and sight-board to make it stand out against the wooded surroundings.

The '5' passes over the high viaduct above the Penrhyn Railway and the River Ogwen and, with tender rearing and tit-tuping, enters Llandegai Tunnel (505 yards) with a anticipatory blast from the hooter. Penrhyn Siding, also a wooded spot, is always of interest, for here the branch to Port Penrhyn curves sharply off to the right throught a five-barred gate. I once saw a '4F' 0-6-0 and train standing on the headshunt by the tunnel's west portal. On the down side, Penrhyn Siding and Bethesda Jn signalboxes had stood within sight of each other, but the former was closed in August 1954. The Bethesda branch, closed to passenger traffic, leaves the main line at an initial 1 in 60 and a warning of the even stiffer climb to come. The branch signals stand at 'on' — a mute testimony to the line's decay.

Leaning out cautiously in Bangor Tunnel (913 yards) we can see the flickering orange radiance cast by the fire on the roof and walls, and then spot the green light of the underslung LNW signal arm at the tunnel mouth. Routed for the down slow line, and with steam shut off and a hollow clangour of coupling rods, we coast to a stand at Platform 3.

My father and I visited Penmaenmawr signalbox

and Bangor shed on several occasions. The box at Penmaenmawr was a modern flat-topped structure opened on 7 December 1953 to replace an LNW box following the 'Irish Mail' smash of August 1950. Mr Thomas, the signalman, was always happy to point out the salient features of block instruments and lever frame which controlled signals showing the development of signalling practice from c1921 to c1955, thus:

Up main
Distant (colour-light).
Nos 1/2 Homes (outer and inner homes) — tall steel posts and Nichols arms.
No 3 Home (starting) — short LNW/LMS wood post with fluted arm (which always bounced four times!).
Starting (advanced starting) — tall, tubular steel post/Nichols arm.
Down main
Distant — LNW in every detail and the last lower-quadrant semaphore at Penmaenmawr.
Outer and Inner Homes — tubular steel post/Nichols arm.
Starting — right-hand bracket/lattice main stem/ steel doll/highly-sprung Nichols arm.
Advanced Starting — LNW/LMS mini-post for visibility beneath bridge with fluted arm.

I was allowed to 'pull off' proudly for an up passenger headed by the superb, but enigmatic, BR '8P' 4-6-2 No 71000 *Duke of Gloucester*, and for a down parcels with Hughes/Fowler '5MT' 2-6-0 No 42885.

As an example of the variety of motive power found along the North Wales Coast, a representative two hours' spotting at Penmaenmawr on 31 August 1961 offered 'WD' 2-8-0 No 90655, Stanier '8F' 2-8-0 No 48667, and Hughes/Fowler 'Crab' 42765 on freights, and 'Jubilee' No 45567 *South Australia*, Class '5s' Nos 45345, 45147, 44682 and Class 40 diesel-electric No D319 on passenger traffic. Class '4F' 0-6-0 No 44525 bunted the steel Catfish wagons in the permanent way sidings. Our trips to Chester produced more exciting finds and greater variety. A composition drawn from several similar journeys includes Midland '4F' 0-6-0 No 43981 emerging from the self-contained low-level yard at Colwyn Bay; Midland '3F' 0-6-0 No 43618 at Rhyl

(on 15 June 1962); ex-Lancashire and Yorkshire '3F' 0-6-0s Nos 52119 (round-top firebox) and 52438 (Belpaire firebox) also at Rhyl; a host of the attractive Stanier '5' 2-6-0s at Mold Junction (including the first, No 42945), and joy at Chester in the form of ex-LNW 'G2A' 0-8-0 No 49094 and 'G2' No 49438. The L and Y 0-6-0 No 52119, with its classic open cab, large dome and tall dignified chimney, was a particular favourite and I found the Belpaire version only a little less pleasing.

Having being held at signals at the head of a long down van train, the LNW '7F' No 49094 made Chester (General) resound to her insistent exhaust as she regained speed, on an occasion that sticks in my memory.

This, then is a brief recall of the North Wales coast main line in the latter-days of steam, a stretch of railway that held such variety in motive power and train working and which nowadays seems to have lost much of its former style and prestige, evidenced by the reduction of most of its four-tracked sections, and a decline in most of its facilities.

Opposite page top: 'Britannia' Pacific No 70048 *The Territorial Army 1908-1958* is clear of Penmaenbach Tunnel with the down 'Irish Mail'.   *Kenneth Field*

Far left: Stanier '5' No 45116 arrives at Bangor with the 13.40 ex-Manchester (Exchange) on 3 August 1964.   *M. Dunnett*

Left: The 'Welsh Dragon' push-pull train moves away from Llandudno Jn towards Llandudno behind BR '2' 2-6-2T No 84003 on 6 August 1962.   *S. D. Wainwright*

Above: The final type of Stanier '5' — No 44687 leaves Prestatyn on an up express on 28 June 1958. *S. D. Wainwright*

Below: The author's favourite L&Y 0-6-0, No 52119, of Rhyl shed, seen shunting at Holywell Jn on 2 June 1961.   *D. Holmes*

The British Columbia Railway

R. M. TUFNELL

Operating wholly in the Canadian province that boasts on its car registration plates 'Beautiful British Columbia', the British Columbia Railway started life in 1912 as the Pacific Great Eastern, but more appropriately could have been called the Pacific Great Northern as it went north and not east.

The curious name arose through a tenuous connection with the former Great Eastern Railway in Britain as much of the debenture issue of $7.5 million was heavily oversubscribed in the City of London.

The Railway had grown out of small beginnings from as far back as 1891. The Vancouver, Westminster and Yukon had built a line from

Vancouver to Westminster (some 15 miles) which is now part of the Burlington Northern system and the Howe Sound, Pemberton Valley and Northern had completed less than 10 miles when it turned to the Government of British Columbia for financial aid.

At this stage the project was taken over by Messrs Foley, Welch and Stewart, then the leading railway construction contractors on the North American continent. Timothy Foley of St Paul, Minnesota; Patrick Welch of Spokane, Washington and John Stewart of Vancouver thus became the promoters and builders of the Pacific Great Eastern which was incorporated on 20 February 1912.

The ultimate object was to reach the Peace River area, 700 miles north of Vancouver, thus providing a north-south route through British Columbia from the Peace River to the Mexican border, but the finance guaranteed by the Province covered only the 480 miles to Prince George.

A press report of October 1912 read 'the erection of construction camps of the PGE will be started next week at Lillooet and before long dirt will be flying . . .' Starting north from Squamish (the original terminus of the Howe Sound, Pemberton Valley and Northern), 40 miles north of Vancouver, by 1915 some 176 miles had been laid and were in use. Twelve and a half miles between North Vancouver and Horseshoe Bay were also in operation.

By 1917 work had started south from Prince George, but there were still three major gaps in the line, between Horseshoe Bay and Squamish, between Koster and Quesnel, and between Cotwood and Stoner, when the contractors declared their financial inability to proceed. An investigation showed that only $40,000 had been received by the Company from sources other than the sale of bonds. The contractors claimed that they were unable to realise on their townsite lands and blamed the war stringency.

In 1918 the Provincial government decided to carry on with the project and the contractor-owners surrendered all their rights. By October 1921 the line from Squamish to Quesnel (348 miles) was in operation, but then the Province decided to delay any further work in view of doubts about the commercial viability of the Railway.

Nothing further was done till 1949 when it was decided to complete the 80-mile section from Quesnel to Prince George to connect with the northern transcontinental line of the Canadian National Railway. This portion was opened for traffic in January 1953.

1956 saw the gap between North Vancouver and Squamish closed and in 1958 extensions were opened to Chetwynd, Fort St John and Dawson Creek. Like many popular railways its initials were translated by humorists to 'Please go Easy', 'Prince George

Eventually', and 'Past God's Endurance', but all that changed in 1972 when the name was changed to British Columbia Railway.

At last the Peace River was linked by rail to the Pacific Coast, and further extensions included a branch from Kennedy to Mackenzie (23 miles) in 1966, a 72-mile extension of the main line, from Odell to Fort St James in 1968 and a further extension of 251 miles from Fort St John to Fort Nelson in 1971. This last extension took the railway close to the Yukon border and provided a main line nearly 1,000 miles long.

Another proposed extension, towards the mineral rich Dease Lake area, has been opened as far as Bulkley House, 206 miles from Odell, but on 5 April 1977 the Provincial Government announced a 'pause' in the remaining construction work. Subsequently the works were abandoned and the contractors paid off.

The first 300 miles contain some of the most spectacular scenery with a 25-mile climb from Cheakamus to Alta Lake (2,100ft) at 2.2% (1 in 45) grades, followed by a similar descent to Mount Currie, a further climb to Birken at 1,615ft and a descent to Lillooet at 793ft. From Lillooet a 31-mile ascent at 2.2% grades brings the line to Hill Top at 3,510ft and a gentle climb takes it to the highest point near Potter at 3,965ft above sea level.

The remaining stretches entirely in hilly or mountainous country through the Cariboo, Telegraph, Misinchinka and Omineka ranges, all included in the generic term 'Rocky Mountains', manage by judicious use of river valleys to avoid grades generally in excess of 1 in 27 except for short stretches of 1 in 60 in the Fort St John and Dawson Creek Subdivisions.

The very names take one back to the pioneer days of the Yukon trail, the Indians and the French settlers, and everywhere the scenery is magnificent. It is a pity that relatively few people will be able to visit the Railway, but a descriptive account of a journey is given by O. S. Nock in his book *Railways of Canada*.

At the end of 1977 the trackage was made up of 1,858 miles (288 of these under construction), but for accounting purposes the lines north from Fort St John and Fort St James are considered still to be in the development stage and the 'established' railway totals 885 miles of main line track. The 250 mile Fort St John-Fort Nelson section was severely damaged by freak weather conditions and, although only opened in 1971, is being considered for closure.

At present, the locomotive fleet consists entirely of units built by Alco (American Locomotive Company) and their successors, now manufactured in Canada by Bombardier-MLW at Montreal. The fleet comprises around 120 locomotives and all, except for three 1,000hp shunters, are classified as 'road switchers' or freight locomotives. The classification system is simply based

Above: Train No 14, southbound from Lillooet to North Vancouver, picking up train orders at Pemberton. Three 3,000hp units are on the front and a further three with slave unit mid-train. *Joe McMillan*

on the rated horsepower, and thus an 'RS20' class locomotive is a 2,000hp road switcher. Several different locomotive designs may thus come within one class. The largest class consists of thirty locomotives classified 'RS30' and comprises five Alco 'Century' '630' locomotives built under licence in Canada and a further twenty 'M630' derivatives incorporating MLW design modifications. The last five have the Canadian-designed 'comfort cab' of advanced specification, and are the only ones of their type to be so fitted. In the 2,000hp bracket the BCR owns eight of the latest Canadian-designed 'M420' locomotives delivered in 1973/4 and a further eight of these supplied to the BCR are cabless 'slave' units, again the only ones of their type.

Late in 1979 the BCR placed an order for ten General Motors SD 40-2 3,000hp diesel locomotives. The 12-wheel SD 40-type is now the most widely used freight locomotive in Canada. The order is the company's first major break in its traditional use of Alco or MLW designs.

For its traffic the railway taps the vast resources of the northern part of British Columbia where the population is too sparse to warrant a passenger service.

Above: Train No 34 on the Prince George sub-division on a new alignment, by-passing the large timber trestle bridge on the right of the photo, at Australian Creek, south of Quesnel. Motive power is MLW C-630 unit No 703 leading Alco C-425 No 804; mid-train are slave units and remote control car. An October 1978 photograph.   *Ken Perry*

Below: Extra 632 North on the Fort St John sub-division with Alco C-420 632 leading RS-3s Nos 562/78, bound for Fort Nelson and seen at Baldonnel on the climb up from the Peace River valley on 26 September 1978.   *Ken Perry*

The five Budd railcars maintain a daily Vancouver-Lillooet passenger working and on alternate days each week this is extended to Prince George or Bulkley House. It carries about 70,000 passengers per year.

On the passenger front, an interesting development in 1979 was the establishment of a Budd railcar service between Prince George and Bulkley House on the Dease Lake line. Later in the year the RDC was replaced by a mixed train with one passenger car formed ahead of the caboose on scheduled freights. Another mixed train commenced operation in the autumn of 1979 to convey school children from Seton Lake to Lillooet.

Forest products in the form of timber, timber-based boards, wood pulp, paper and wood chips for paper-making form the largest part of the Company's freight traffic amounting in 1975 to some 68%. Minerals are plentiful in this region and the railway carries quantities of metal ores, sulphur and other mineral concentrates as well as grain and farm produce from the Peace River area. There is also a sizeable 'piggy-bank' traffic in articulated trailers which are off-loaded at the northern points for onward truck haulage over the Alaska Highway, a dirt road into the far north. Private industries served by carload shipments number some 700, the principal ones being at Vancouver, Prince George and Williams Lake. The Company's freight car stock numbers 9,322, made up of 5,518 boxcars, 3,406 flats, 1,232 chip gondolas and 427 refrigerator cars with a balance of 250 miscellaneous vehicles.

Financially, the railway made an operating profit right up to 1973, but depreciation and interest have now turned this into a nett loss. The deficit began to rise fast after 1973, when the oil price escalation affected so much of the free world's economy. This is also reflected in the costs of such items as rolling stock where, for instance, the average North American cost of a boxcar rose from $7,515 in 1955, to $14,610 in 1965 and to $31,166 in 1975.

In an endeavour to keep the rolling stock costs down a freight car manufacturing plant was set up alongside the main workshops at Squamish, as a separate division with the name of Railwest Manufacturing Company. Production started in 1975 and the output was intended to be 1,000 cars per annum.

However, the plant produced 247 woodchip gondolas in 1975, 153 woodchip gondolas and 532 bulkhead flatcars in 1976 and 368 bulkhead flats and 100 open top hopper cars in 1977, before being closed.

The line as a whole employed 5,183 people during 1976 with a wages bill in that year of $49.6 million, but as so many of the jobs are seasonal, the average level of employment in the peak summer months is just over 3,000. The employees are divided among seven trade unions who come together under a joint council.

Above: A Budd RDC-3 forming a northbound passenger train at North Vancouver. *BCR*

Below: Train No 12 leaving Squamish with three M-630s providing power, in March 1974. *Ken Perry*

The Railway is probably unique in being the only substantial operation in the North American continent that is equipped entirely with Alco-type locomotives. This arose quite by chance in that the first of the Company's diesel locomotives were of this make and it stayed with Alco designs until 1979. It also had one Fairbanks-Morse 1,000hp switcher built in 1949 and acquired on lease in 1969, but this was retired in 1975. Seven small GE diesels of 1948/50 vintage were all sold off by 1964.

The existing fleet consists mainly of locomotives purchased direct from Montreal Locomotive Works, which acquired the Alco designs when Alco ceased new locomotive building, and some bought second hand from United States railroads where these have been sold after corporate mergers. The latter are given a thorough overhaul in the BCR works at Squamish and the engines are derated by 10% thereby ensuring a longer life and power matching with existing locomotives.

The twelve 2,500hp Alco Model 'C425' units

purchased by the BCR in 1976 are their most recent acquisition. These had been in service on the Erie Lackawanna Railroad for ten years when sold to the BCR. The first of these to be put through the shops was painted in BCR two-tone green using an epoxy-based paint. The extra cost of this finish was estimated at only $650 over conventional paint and it is hoped that this will give an additional two years to the paint life.

Apart from these 2,500hp locomotives, the Company's last purchase of 3,000hp locomotives (Nos 705-30) and all the 2,000hp models have the latest MLW — DOFASCO bogies. The two-axle bogies are of the Metalastik 'Zero Weight Transfer' type and the three-axle units are the 'HI-ADD' type, having no bolster or centreplate. The vertical loads are transmitted through four laminated rubber elements with snubbing and swivelling limiting stops.

The British Columbia Railway now makes regular use of Locotrol for radio control of locomotives placed within the train. Although the system can give the head-end engineer independent driving control of the remote locomotives, automatic multiple working with the head-end is adopted as standard. Thirteen of the 3,000hp locos have head-end or master Locotrol systems. Eight 2,000hp RCL cabless locomotives and three engineless remote control cars, which are old cabless passenger unit bodies, have the receiving or slave system. The RCLs and RCCs will operate in multiple directly with other units as required.

BCR's experience with this remote control equipment made by the Radiation Inc Control Division has been very satisfactory, but some operators have not been so fortunate. The Burlington Northern had some nasty moments with theirs when the slave units which

should have been braking were still under power on a down grade, and this was not very comforting to the train crew! This happened in the Stevens Pass where the Cascade Tunnel takes the line through the mountains between Seattle and Wenatchee. It was thought that the tunnel may have affected the signals between the control locomotive and the slave units, but whatever the reason BN have now ceased to use this system.

Assignment of motive power and train scheduling falls under the Chief Train Dispatcher. Single track, severe grades and the distance between the main shops require continuous optimisation of train dispatches and train tonnages. Although there are typical patterns of working, almost any casual visitor to the Railway will see other variations. Between North Vancouver and Prince George the heaviest traffic is southwards. Trains are typically brought down with two head-end units of 3,000hp and two midtrain units incorporating an RCL or an RCC. At Lillooet two more units with a crew attach to the rear and push either to Mons or through to Squamish, depending on the next shop service or north train.

Northbound from North Vancouver units are not generally placed within the train and RCLs can be seen in the head-end consist. Car coupler strength limits what should be done at the head end but three or four of the largest locomotives giving up to 12,000hp are sometimes used.

The BCR also operates the restored CPR 'Royal Hudson' 4-6-4 No 2860 now owned by the Government of BC which runs excursions in the summer months between Vancouver and Squamish. This is stabled at the North Vancouver shed and kept in beautiful condition.

During his visit the writer was made very welcome by Mr G. L. Kelly, the Chief Mechanical Officer of BCR, to whom thanks are due for his kind co-operation and for data and photographs supplied.

Below: Freight and passenger motive power in sidings at Lillooet. *BCR*

By the Great Northern lineside

R. A. H. WEIGHT

R. A. H. Weight was the doyen of a large group of railway enthusiasts who followed the developments and activities of the Great Northern Railway and the LNER (Southern Area) and contributed much to the popularity of the GN main line in the steam era. This article was submitted for publication in 1967, but for reasons of length was destined not to appear in Railway World. *With the Stirling Singles and 2-4-0s and the Ivatt Atlantics now growing dim in living memory it seems appropriate to recall a memorable Railway and to honour a railway recorder of the highest quality.*

The Great Northern was one of the chief medium-sized English railways, one of the late-comers among the early Victorian undertakings, having established its direct Kings Cross-Doncaster trunk route in 1852. Its history and importance as the southern partner in the triple alliance of companies operating the East Coast route to Scotland, together with its extensive secondary or branch lines in the London suburbs and Home Counties, East Midlands and the West Riding, have been described elsewhere. The GNR created and retained a reputation for speed, and for the high standard of its principal express services. Stirling's eight-foot Singles and Ivatt's large Altantics captured popular imagination, figuring in numerous illustra-

Above: A Leeds-Kings Cross express passing Oakleigh Park behind Ivatt large Atlantic No 1451. *LPC*

tions, children's books or advertisements and the like.

In 1909 we moved into a house north of Wood Green station, $5\frac{1}{3}$ miles from Kings Cross, closely overlooking the five-track main lines and sidings, with the down Enfield line flying junction over them used also by many empty stock trains. A little further away we could see the up Enfield track and the branch nearly as far as Bowes Park station; Bounds Green carriage sidings and signalbox; and, more distantly, the siding extremities of the GER Palace Gates branch terminal. Within that orbit some 500 train and engine movements were ordinarily dealt with in a 24hr period, gradually increasing through the heyday peacetime years up to 1914. This was the time when railway companies enjoyed almost a monopoly with longer distance inland transport.

Nearly *all* the GNR locomotives were painted lined-out green and were usually kept clean. The older, more modestly powered ones of Stirling design, built 1870-96 and 'much of a muchness' (of 4-2-2, 2-2-2, 2-4-0, 0-4-2, 0-6-0; 0-4-4 well and side tank, 0-6-0ST types) were in many cases being rebuilt with more effective Ivatt domed boilers, or withdrawn. Stirling's Singles, the 0-4-2s and passenger tanks were destined to remain in service a while longer and were being

65

Left: A typical GNR 'Parly', headed by Stirling 8ft Single No 1008 and rebuilt Stirling 2-4-0 No 752. The train is the 14.20 Kings Cross-Cambridge and Peterborough. *Eric Neve Collection*

Bottom: Ivatt 4-4-2T No 1505 at Belle Isle with a down local train formed of four-wheeled stock and 'birdcage' brakes making up a typical set train.
Rixon Bucknall Collection/Ian Allan Library

Right: Ivatt 4-4-2T No 1516 near Crouch End with a local train for Alexandra Palace. *W. J. Reynolds*

removed to country depots, so they were seen less or disappeared entirely from the London area.

Ivatt domed engines at work in the early 1910s comprised 2-4-0s, Nos 1061-70; 4-4-2s and 4-4-0s, small and large boilered; inside-cylinder 4-2-2s; 0-8-0s; 5ft 8in mixed traffic 0-6-0s, Nos 1-15, and the several series of 5ft 2in 0-6-0s. There were also the ubiquitous and long-lived 0-6-0STs.

The varnished teak passenger rolling stock to be seen included ECJS (East Coast Joint Stock) coaches, dining and sleeping cars fitted with Westinghouse as well as standard GN vacuum brakes. There were a good many twelve-wheeled corridor vehicles giving a distinctive-sounding and comfortable ride including restaurant or sleeping cars, both Joint and GN stock. Clerestory roofs were as common as on other railways although the impressive new-style Gresley elliptical roofed, bow ended main line stock with buckeye couplings was coming into service, destined to be standardised and further developed later by the LNER. Three-coach sets of attractively equipped elliptical coaches with lavatory accommodation, but not vestibuled, were used for a long while on services between Kings Cross and Cambridge, Grimsby, Leeds and Manchester.

There were also older and smaller bogie coaches, eight-wheeled non-bogie, numerous rather rigid but comfortable six-wheelers, also six-wheeled kitchen cars, guard's, parcels and Post Office vans. Gas lighting was still in considerable use. Gresley's articulation, familiar afterwards on a much more extensive scale, had begun to turn pairs of six-wheelers, including some ECJS examples, into one smoother riding twin bogie unit.

Looming large in the picture, the heavy London suburban traffic was catered for almost entirely by close-coupled set trains of eleven (a few were twelve) short four-wheelers — second-class at the London end, first in the centre, and third at the country end comprising rather more than half the total accommodation. All compartments were upholstered to a greater or lesser extent but provided rather spartan and straight-backed travel. From 1912 eight-coach bogie sets similarly classed gradually replaced the four-wheelers and provided the luxury of steam heating! At first the new sets were formed of four 'twins', afterwards converted to two 'quadruplets' articulated. Being a great deal heavier these rather overtaxed the neat and attractive Ivatt 4-4-2Ts as most of the start to stop timings were tight and there were gradients as steep as 1 in 60 up from Finsbury Park to Highgate with tougher short stretches. In any case, the Ivatt 0-6-2Ts, blessed with greater adhesion, were gradually taking over. Even so, the link of 10 well-kept 4-4-2Ts at Hornsey shed continued unaltered up to 1913/4 — some time after the allocation of 35 tank engines at Kings Cross Top Shed had normally consisted entirely of 0-6-2Ts.

There were two sets of men for each locomotive working shifts up to 10hr, through a daily changed sequence of turns: 28 at Kings Cross and eight at Hornsey. Some diagrams involved mileages up to 200-210; running chimney-first northbound, bunker leading on return. The engines were supposed to be in shed for washing out and examination every fifth working day. The furthest they went on the main line was Hatfield, with a couple of branch trips thence to Luton; they ran to Cuffley when the Enfield branch had been extended that far, also on the branches from Finsbury Park to High Barnet, Alexandra Palace and (mostly as a local Finchley shuttle service) to Edgware.

The suburban passenger tanks worked midday and night freight trains via the Metropolitan Widened Lines, Snow Hill and Ludgate Hill and beyond on devious routes on what is now the SR to and from Herne Hill, Hither Green, Battersea and Feltham. They were also used on van, horsebox or special train transfer trips. The connecting single-line tunnels between the suburban platforms at Kings Cross Main

(York Road, up, and 'B', later No 16 down) were severely graded. It was sometimes a sulphurous struggle to get up the 1 in 35/48 to the GN station from Kings Cross, Met through Hotel Curve tunnel, and tricky to restart a crowded train from Platform 16. Through trains from Moorgate Met using this route were very frequent during peak hours as the traffic intensified, and some did not make a call at Kings Cross Suburban. Until 1915 they ran also on Sundays. Destination boards were displayed on the front of smokebox or bunker. In addition to Kings Cross station shunting work the 4-4-2Ts and 0-6-2Ts carrying headboards 'Nos 1-5 EC' or '1-3S' (Shunt) hauled main line and other empty trains to and from Bounds Green, Hornsey, Finsbury Park or Holloway Carriage Sidings; such round trips often occupying 2-3hr, including reversing and waiting in yards, for signals, and perhaps for a lengthy period at the buffer stops while the outward expresses were loading. Two Stirling 0-4-4Ts, Nos 767/931, lingered on for a long time as carriage pilots fitted with Westinghouse brake for handling 'foreign' stock.

By now controlled by the LNWR, numerous North London Railway Broad Street trains traversed GN suburban routes as far as Potters Bar, Gordon Hill (with one to Cuffley), High Barnet, Alexandra Palace, and provided an all-day service. They were antiquated-looking outfits but seemed to go on and on! Third-class carriages had no upholstery and only low dividing partitions between compartments. There were three classes as in GN sets. Short wooden guards' vans at each end had an elevated look-out window in the roof. Early in our period there were a few of the 1869 design, inside-cylinder 4-4-0Ts still about. The stout little Adams-Park outside cylinder 4-4-0Ts continued to be the mainstay of the NL services for many years.

Living at Wood Green until well into the LNER period, I established a 'recording station' which probably became quite unique as with the aid of relatives, railwaymen and friends a fairly complete record was maintained night and day of the passing locomotives and traffic from 1910/11, with times and loads whenever possible and, often in later years, drivers' names. As a result, I became thoroughly familiar with the timings, rosters and engine allocations which were little changed over a long period.

I had left the 'rival' Midland Railway's service and after a period of commercial training joined the headquarters staff of one of the big shipping companies, on whose behalf I made a good many train travels as well as some by sea; meanwhile becoming more and more wholeheartedly a railway enthusiast.

In 1909 LNW 'Precursor' 4-4-0 No 412 *Marquis* worked on a short period of trials between Doncaster-Kings Cross and back alternatively with GN Atlantic, No 1451. The latter showed a slight superiority in coal consumption and mean speed but as the average train load was only about 240 tons tare it was not a severe task for those unsuperheated engines. They came up with a light semi-fast; back on the 17.45 Leeds 'Diner'. In return, Ivatt Atlantic No 1449 ran Euston-Crewe and back with heavier trains on an easier road and seemed to manage all right. The first superheated GN small Atlantic, No 988, painted shop grey, working from Peterborough on extended trials on 20 July 1910, was on the (Newcastle) express arriving in Kings Cross at 13.40 returning at 15.00. This was a regular Peterborough-Doncaster-Kings Cross (non-stop)-Peterborough turn with the same crew. Next day the Newcastle train came up, late, headed by the Vulcan Foundry 4-cyl compound 4-4-2, No 1300 which the GN ordered as an outside venture to compare with their two experimental compound, and ordinary,

Atlantics. The compounds were seldom put on the hardest turns and petered out as such before or just after grouping.

Unfortunately I have no photographs of any — lineside pictures then being rare — but 4-2-2 'eight-footers' having large outside cylinders and long connecting rods, and other 'Singles' passed on express goods or fish trains with 28 wagons as a maximum. The GN was developing fast, with fully braked freight and produce services being formed mainly of covered wagons known as red vans, or rather similar grey and white vans for perishable traffic. At first the only modern mixed traffic locomotives were the 'No 1' class 0-6-0s of which three, Nos 7-9, were stationed in London; they were employed on long goods runs, Kings Cross-Cambridge expresses and some general main-line work. The superheated version, LNER Class 'J2', Nos 71-80, three at Kings Cross shed, shared in all such duties including a York-London night freight hitherto handled by larger-boilered 4-4-0s, LNER Class 'D2'. Before World War 1 the latter shared in almost every kind of haulage from expresses to empty wagons.

Coal traffic was heavy. 0-8-0s in original form barked loudly on loads up to 60 wagons. Stirling or Ivatt 0-6-0s were on them, too, with 45-50 wagons. Northward long return empties' trains from the busy Ferme Park Sidings, Hornsey, often run as extras, were also worked by Atlantics, 4-4-0s and 2-4-0s returning 'unbalanced' to Peterborough. Not infrequently it was a long struggle up the long 1 in 200 rise to Potters Bar with intermediate signal stops, including one in front of my old house on the now defunct goods line terminating at Wood Green Tunnel Box.

I shall be including a survey of typical main line and locomotive operating on summer days in 1913. A notable enterprise before that was the 'Bradford Special' put on at short notice from 11 July 1910, consisting of four coaches including a composite dining car, timed from Kings Cross to Doncaster in 165-166min and to Bradford in 3hr 40min via Wakefield; the quickest so far as I remember in GN days or for a long while after. It provided a last fling on fast runs non-stop to and from Doncaster for Kings Cross Ivatt 4-2-2, No 263, and 2-2-2s, Nos 872/76, which shared the duty with 4-4-0s, Nos 49/50. On this turn, they left Kings Cross at 14.15, arriving back at 22.05 with second link crews. The reason for the 'Bradford Special' was that the Midland had put on faster through portion services between St Pancras and Bradford (Exchange) — the GN-L&Y station — via Sheffield and Thornhill. These took over 4 hours, with other services by that or the normal route into the Midland station via Leeds occupying longer, so the Great Northern's premier position in the London-West Riding passenger field was not seriously challenged though they felt hurt! In spring 1912, after a miners' strike caused curtailment of services, the 'Bradford Specials' were not reinstated. They had provided some lively running but patronage was light as they followed so soon after the long established 13.30 departure, and 21.25 arrival at Kings Cross.

All the remaining GN Singles worked from provincial depots thereafter, mainly in Lincolnshire. Apart from preserved No 1, they disappeared before or during the 1914-18 war. A few came up sometimes to Kings Cross until early in 1914 on night fish trains or extras, returning, say, with the 05.20 slow or at busy times on the second part of the 10.35 or summer 13.05 with through coaches to Grimsby or the

M&GN line. They were eight-footers or the more graceful 7ft 7½in Ivatt 4-2-2s. One astonishing morning two of the latter, Nos 265/70, went home to Peterborough coupled, light engines!

On 31 March 1913, the first part of the express due Kings Cross at 13.05 consisting of the Grimsby portion with extra vehicles from Skegness, bogies and 6-wheelers, quite 260 tons full, was surprisingly and, for the last time, hauled from Peterborough by No 1003 of the final Stirling series, built 1894 though looking much older. The load was a bit too much and some time had been lost. Partly due to the old-time brakes seizing and partly due to the weight of the train on the short rise from the dip under the Regents Canal in Gasworks Tunnel, the veteran stalled within sight of the platforms with part of her train still in the tunnel. Restarting efforts proving of no avail, 'N1' 0-6-2T No 1567 was attached in front bunker-first and following combined splutterings pulled the whole outfit into No 1 Platform; 1003 appeared short of steam and water. The driver was a youngish man with perhaps little experience of handling Singles on such a duty. I was there and can still see it all in my mind's eye! The lighter (Leeds) second part, worked from Doncaster by the latest Atlantic No 1461, was badly held up so there was a row!

By Christmas 1910, the long line of 93 large Atlantics had been completed when Nos 1458-61 brought up the Kings Cross allocation to 22. They were of the last superheated batch fitted with 20in dia cylinders, instead of 18¾in, piston valves in place of balanced slide ones and modified boiler content providing 40 tons adhesion weight on the driving wheels — leading after other modernisation to much finer performance by the Atlantics.

Left: LNWR 'Precursor' 4-4-0 No 412 *Marquis* on trials on the GN main line in 1909. The three leading coaches of its train are Gresley GNR corridor vehicles.

Above: A typical GN coal train approaching Potters Bar with Ivatt 'Long Tom' 0-8-0 No 425. *LPC*

Right: The 14.15 Kings Cross-Bradford 'special' climbs to Potters Bar summit behind Stirling 2-2-2 No 872, as rebuilt by Ivatt. *E. Neve*

3 April 1911, saw the debut in London of an upstanding, piston valve, superheated 4-4-0 in shop grey finish, No 51, heading the 17.45 Yorkshire express back to Doncaster, running very quietly. This heralded the last 4-4-0 (LNER 'D1') class of 15 engines numbered 51-65. Nos 59-62 came to Kings Cross shed, 51-55 were allocated to Copley Hill, Leeds, thence taking fast freights to London for a time, also coming through with excursions or reliefs. With the same boiler the '521' class of 5ft 2in 0-6-0 began its invaluable general service, being increased eventually to 110 locomotives by 1922.

Henry Ivatt retired in September 1911, having added to stock in 16 years over 700 locomotives and at least 10 new classes of growing power and efficiency during a period of heavy demand and expansion when traffic, loads and speeds were continuing to increase. The GNR directors immediately appointed Mr Gresley, their comparatively little-known Carriage and Wagon Superintendent to succeed him. So began a momentous 30-year career at Doncaster, including for 18 years departmental command of the LNER.

After some delay, on 3 October 1912, Gresley's pioneer small-boilered 2-6-0, No 1630, made her first normal service trip with the 17.10 semi-fast Kings Cross-Baldock. The high framing and Walschaerts gear showed that a new era had begun as a stepping stone to much greater things. She was given a stiff trial with 57 wagons on fast goods timings from Finsbury Park and Peterborough with the NER's dynamometer car, requiring an average speed of about 45-50mile/h. The maximum load so far had been 45 wagons for Atlantics. By 1914 the second Mogul stage was being developed with the introduction of No 1640 with a much larger 5ft 6in dia boiler and two outside cylinders 20in × 26in actuated through 10in piston valves. Some other components were the same as on the first ten which were eventually rebuilt to conform. By 1921 the later Mogul design had grown to 65 engines numbered 1640-704. Being the largest and most effective mixed traffic locomotives so far, they were soon working nearly all the express goods and fish trains, secondary passenger workings and expresses at busy times. As war conditions changed the scene, they were invaluable for hospital, troop or supply specials. Nos 1630-9 were concentrated at provincial sheds, the first five having been initially at Kings Cross.

In GN days until the 1920-30s Kings Cross station had considerably less platform accommodation. There were only three full-length arrival platforms, at least one of which, No 5, had at times to be used for departures. Nos 3/4 were two short stepped sections of what was later 4; 3 being a bay terminating north of the footbridge and taken out of use. There were just two main departure platforms, later Nos 6 and 10, with a group of carriage sidings in-between which the LNER removed except for one when building island Platform 7/8. The space later occupied by Platforms 14/15 in the adjoining local station on the west side was the site of the cramped Loco Yard with turntable and coal stage. Old gasworks buildings stood where the more spacious Loco Yard was later so there were no tracks west of the down slow departure line. A road bridge hindering observation spanned all the lines close to the outer ends of the platforms which were lengthened under LNER auspices, after its removal. Up passenger trains were not often run into the departure platforms, or into the local station. As a result, much empty running, or shunting in and out of the all-too-adjacent Gasworks Tunnel was involved. The working was normally carried through with little delay though the number of long-distance trains was only about half the total of BR days and they were not usually run close together.

Holloway station, 1½ miles from Kings Cross (closed in 1915 and later demolished) just at the summit of the climb at 1 in 105-110 up through the tunnels from the terminus, was a good vantage point for seeing and hearing all-out efforts by various types of locomotive, together with fire or spark throwing which in the case of some of the old Stirlings sometimes went on right up to Potters Bar. The up platform was an island between the fast and slow tracks; the down was served by No 2 slow, an additional passenger line extending from Holloway South to the north end of Wood Green, with the main goods line and carriage sidings to the left.

Signalboxes on the main line were of characteristic, though not particularly prepossessing, appearance, largely constructed of wood. There were separate down and up cabins in some cases almost facing one another: at Kings Cross, Harringay, Hornsey, Cemetery (north of New Southgate), Oakleigh Park, New Barnet South, and 'Twentieth Mile'. The last were located, as the name indicates, as block posts about 2¼ miles north of Hatfield before the single lines to Dunstable and Hertford branched away respectively west and east, long before Welwyn Garden City was heard of. In the two-track 2¾-mile bottleneck north of New Barnet through Hadley Wood to Potters Bar (as well as Greenwood where the slow lines converged until BR days) there were small intermediate boxes at Hadley Wood, Ganwick and Mimms, providing short sections until the LNER introduced automatic colour lights. In later days, semaphore, or colour-light automatic, intermediate block, or long-distance manually-operated signals replaced a number of other cabins down the line. Especially when 'off', and decidedly into the lower quadrant, there was no mistaking the GNR somersault signals pivoted on a bar projected at right angles to the posts.

Compared with the range of hourly or two-hourly high speed expresses of BR days, there was a rather thin and leisurely service of principal trains from Kings Cross in 1913. By day there were trains to Edinburgh at 10.00 and 14.20 only, with summer extras

Left: The final Ivatt passenger design — superheated 4-4-0 No 56, at Kings Cross shed.
Rixon Bucknall Collection/Ian Allan Library

Right: Gresley 2-cyl 2-6-0 No 1637 approaches Hadley Wood with coal empties for Peterborough. *E. Neve*

from 1 July to 30 September, at 09.50 and 11.20, taking $8\frac{1}{4}$hr or more. These also provided the service to Newcastle with the addition of the 17.30. The 11.20 (summer), 14.20 and 17.30 were the only fast through trains to Darlington. There were very semi-fast ones from Kings Cross at 10.35 and Edinburgh at 10.25, taking over 10 hours. There were expresses to Leeds and the West Riding calling (at least) at Peterborough, Doncaster, Wakefield, Holbeck, at 07.15, 10.10, 13.30, 16.00, 17.45; the 13.30 being the quickest, to Leeds in 3hr 42min, just 1hr longer than in 1967, and to Doncaster, in 2hr 54min. The fastest to York was 3hr 35min by the 17.30. Two or three night sleeping car services were allowed $7\frac{3}{4}$hr to Edinburgh conveying through cars to Aberdeen, Inverness, Fort William, etc. Other best times were: Peterborough 82min by the 10.10 and Grantham, 116min by the 03.00 and 18.05.

Southward passengers fared in some ways better all the year as there was an 07.45 restaurant car train ex-Edinburgh, departing at 10.28 from Newcastle, at about 11.15 from Darlington, to arrive at Kings Cross at 16.10; the 10.00 (summer second train 10.10) from Edinburgh called at Darlington. Night southbound Scottish trains, however, were not so fast as northbound, so the 10.00 and its summer duplicate were the quickest in $8\frac{1}{4}$hr, the 1896-1932 agreed daytime minimum schedule. In general, the up main line service roughly balanced the down. Nearly all, except principal expresses stopped at Finsbury Park for ticket collection; a good many northbound also called.

Each way several through semi-fast Leeds or York trains or portions provided numerous intermediate and branch connections then in greater demand. Main line slows which shunted and waited at principal stations to connect into and out of faster trains served all stations between, say, Hatfield and Doncaster. These calls totalled 36; in 1967 only 13 stations remained open. To and from Kings Cross the slows were hauled by a variety of engines from Atlantics to 2-4-0s or 0-6-0s, occasional Singles, and Moguls when they became more numerous. Several separate fastish Cambridge trains ran each way and were allowed 79-89 minutes. There were a few other daily summer-only expresses, and certain-day and Saturday extras; in addition a good many were run unadvertised.

One of the few daily crack trains described in the timetable as 'Special . . . Express' was the popular 13.37 ex-Bradford; 14.00 Leeds (reverse), Wakefield (attach Huddersfield coach) depart 14.21; making the longest GN non-stop run thence to Kings Cross: $175\frac{3}{4}$ miles in 186min, an average speed of 56.7mile/h). This was due in at 17.27 working time, advertised as 17.25, in 3hr 25min from Leeds, so being about 15min quicker than any other Leeds service to and from Kings Cross or St Pancras. The load was never more than six vehicles, or just over 200 tons, but it had one of the best timekeeping records, being worked by a Kings Cross Atlantic. With the same crew this had worked down to Leeds at 07.15. This gave a 372-mile duty of over 11hrs, the crew receiving the then maximum mileage payment equal to one day's pay — driver 8s (40p)!

The fastest booking — an average start to stop of 57.5mile/h — was from Grantham at 17.58 with $105\frac{1}{2}$ miles run in 110min. This applied to the four-coach 'Special' a last survivor of the once competitive, separate Manchester-Kings Cross expresses. It was allowed 4hr 8min from Manchester London Road and 2hr 58min from Sheffield, so providing one of the quickest services from the Cutlery City by any route.

Turning now to the promised survey of the main line in the summer of 1913, the only down express I never saw, though heard sometimes, was the 03.00 to York and Leeds, a fast, light train run more for newspapers than passengers. It was one of the daily Doncaster and back Kings Cross Atlantic and mens' workings. The

Above: The 4-cyl compound Atlantic No 292, built Doncaster 1905. *LPC*

others were with the 10.10, and non-stop on easy timings with the 09.50 and 11.20 summer Scottish trains. The last of these was hauled forward by another Doncaster Atlantic without a stop to Harrogate via Knottingley L&Y, and Church Fenton, returning with the corresponding up express which came the same way but was non-stop to Grantham where a Grantham 4-4-2 took over. The Doncaster engine went home on the 20.08, which was a continuation of the 16.20 semi-fast Kings Cross-Leeds. The 13.40 from Kings Cross included a restaurant car portion for Harrogate using the same direct route avoiding Leeds — continued for many years by the LNER. As there were one or two other through coaches that way a GN 4-4-0 was stationed at Starbeck shed, Harrogate. The 13.40 was taken out by a Peterborough Atlantic, as was the summer 13.05 formed on Tuesday, Thursday, Saturday of smart maroon NER elliptical roofed stock including restaurant cars, through to Scarborough, Whitby and West Hartlepool. Alternatively, the 13.05 was made up of newly painted GN stock, as were the last two coaches on the 13.05 run daily to Cromer, detached at Peterborough and then hustled over the difficult M&GN line by an umber or yellow 4-4-0. This portion took considerably longer than the best GE trains from Liverpool Street, but was quicker than the all-year 15.00 through from Kings Cross to Kings Lynn, Norwich, Cromer and Mundesley, which detached an old-stock portion at Hitchin, booked non-stop on to Cambridge.

The 15.25, headed by a Doncaster Atlantic that had come through from Leeds arriving at 13.55, called at Peterborough and principal stations and had an L&Y through coach for Accrington and Blackburn in front, taken by a GN locomotive from Doncaster via Wakefield Kirkgate, as far as Halifax. It also had a

portion for Harrogate via Church Fenton, and for York going forward to Newcastle, but no restaurant car. Nor had the 16.00, formed of non-vestibuled elliptical roofed stock through to Leeds, Bradford, Sheffield and Grimsby, taken out by a Grantham 4-4-2, as was the 18.05 'Special Dining Car Express' to Hull. The main portion of this arrived at 22.12, and the Manchester coaches were due at 22.20. In earlier years this had been a Manchester train only. A Great Central 4-4-0 usually worked the 18.05 from Grantham to Retford, thence on to Sheffield with the Manchester coaches.

The dining car for the 15.40 express ex-Manchester went down the previous day on the 12.30 Kings Cross-Sheffield, and then on empty apparently, exemplifying some of the lightly loaded services operated in those days for competitive reasons or to provide through fast trains to and from a few intermediate towns.

The down early evening country businessmens' trains were fewer and much different compared with the 1960s. For example, the 16.30 for Potters Bar, Hatfield (set back from down main to single line branch on up side) and stations to Hertford (GN), was worked by a 4-4-2T succeeding many years' use of Stirling 0-4-4Ts. The 17.00 was non-stop to Hitchin in 40min where it divided into three trains. Frequently it left Kings Cross double-headed by a Cambridge 2-4-0 or 4-4-0 leading a Kings Cross superheated 4-4-0 with a mixed bag of 11-13 vehicles. On arrival at Hitchin, the front locomotive moved off out of the way and the train engine left at once with the first three coaches for Royston and Cambridge — reached in 75min, and the fastest timing to the University city. I believe that a Hitchin 4-4-0, of the '1073' class, took the centre section for Huntingdon, Holme, Peterborough, Essendine, Stamford; going on light or with empty stock to Grantham for an up fish train. The rear portion, all stations to Cambridge, was taken by the locomotive that had been in front from London.

The 17.49 was partly for Hitchin, and the remainder for Luton and Dunstable, serving all stations from Hadley Wood. The 18.18 called at all stations between Hitchin and Huntingdon, after Hatfield, and was worked by a Kings Cross 4-4-0 or 0-6-0 which ran from Huntingdon to St Ives ($5\frac{1}{2}$ miles along the GN&GE Joint line), to work a freight load of Fenland vegetables and produce back to East Goods Yard, Finsbury Park.

There was a curious 09.20 fast to Hatfield formed of small main line stock for the Dunstable branch, normally worked by an Atlantic which went on light to Hitchin and stood there as main line pilot until returning with the 17.23 up slow unless called upon in emergency as occasionally happened. Hot-boxes were a trouble in those days!

From my ledgers I have selected a few interesting train working items and unusual features from peak summer Saturdays in 1913 when there might easily be 15-20 specials and duplicates, and much late running. On one occasion, the Huddersfield and Halifax portion of the 13.55 arrival Leeds express ran separately for some reason consisting of two 12-wheeled corridors and a small bogie, being brought up from Peterborough by Ivatt Single No 265 which returned on the

Above: Large Atlantic No 1417 passes Greenwood Box with the 15.25 Kings Cross-York; through L&Y coach to Blackburn behind the engine. *LPC*

Below: London-Scarborough summer express at Potters Bar, with the first four vehicles being NER flat-sided corridor stock in maroon livery. The locomotive is Ivatt 4-4-0 No 1339. *E. Neve*

15.45 Yarmouth excursion formed by a suburban set of four-wheeled coaches. The relief to the 15.55 semi-fast arrival was similarly composed and had Stirling Single No 1004 which went back light engine; so did No 25A, a Stirling 0-4-2 from Hatfield which came up with the Dunstable portion ahead of the Hitchin vehicles on the 17.09 arrival. The following week this happened again but the little veteran went home on the 18.18 coupled in front of superheated 0-6-0 No 72, the only time I saw such an odd combination! A sister 0-6-0, No 77, went down with the second part of the 15.25 express with 8 on, including two six-wheelers. Another Saturday this train had 11 coaches with two four-wheeled oddments on the rear, headed by 0-6-0 No 78 piloting 4-4-0 No 1377. Both were stationed at New England, Peterborough.

On the first Saturday in August, when for the Bank

Holiday weekend there were widespread period excursion bookings and generally heavy traffic, well over 30 extras passed me. The 4-4-0s were working more expresses unaided, there were also a few 2-4-0s and one or two '521' class 0-6-0s (LNER 'J6') on slows.

Double heading was not allowed in any circumstances if an Atlantic was booked for a train so at summer weekends the 4-4-2s tackled heavy loads for those days. They had nothing like so much in reserve as afterwards when they had been generally modernised by the LNER. The 15.58 arrival, for instance, from Whitby, Scarborough, Saltburn, had 13 coaches including several 12-wheelers, well over 400 tons full and brought up by a Doncaster Atlantic calling at Peterborough on a fairly easy timing. The fast 13.30 down Leeds had 12 on including a bogie TPO, as regularly run on several day expresses to and from Yorkshire; this train also formed a round trip for a Doncaster engine. The Bank Holiday Friday night period excursion to Edinburgh and Glasgow was loaded to 14, some of these being lighter NE bogies.

A summer Saturday 12 noon departure, first stop Doncaster, was a Polytechnic inclusive eight-day tour to Scotland which chartered an ECJS train including an elderly restaurant or kitchen car used during the

Below: An up outer suburban train passes Oakleigh Park with Ivatt mixed traffic 0-6-0 No 8 as motive power.
Rixon Bucknall Collection/Ian Allan Library

week for scenic day runs on the NB lines from Edinburgh. The return of the tour train was at 08.45 from Waverley the next Saturday, due at Kings Cross at 17.06.

Kings Cross was the base for some astonishingly cheap excursions to the East Coast. The 3s (15p) half-day trips to Skegness — 262 miles or over 7 miles for 1d — were probably the biggest bargain regularly offered up to 1914. This was in a corridor train booked to call only at Spalding for water each way and taking 3hr, or just under, hauled by an Atlantic, such as I sampled comfortably several times. On very busy days, however, it depended upon which portion you were able to get into!

On August Bank Holiday 1913 there was indeed a rush with people booking and queueing in hundreds from 09.00 for an advertised Skegness departure at 11.30, also run on summer Sundays and Thursdays. Variously powered and composed specials left as follows between 10.05 and 11.35:

(1) Large 4-4-2	No 1440:	two four-wheeled suburban sets, 22 coaches
(2) Large 4-4-2	No 1427:	10 corridors, 1 six-wheeler
(3) Large 4-4-2	No 300:	2 bogie local sets (8 twins)
(4) Small 4-4-2	No 253:	11 corridors
(5) Small 2-6-0	No 1630:	10 corridors
(6) Mixed Traffic 0-6-0	No 74:	2 bogie local sets
(7) Superheated 4-4-0	No 59:	11 corridors, 1 six-wheeler
(8) Superheated 4-4-0	No 62:	mixed stock

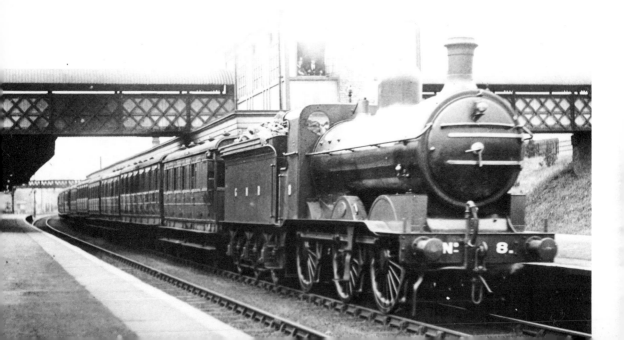

Several of the total loads would be about 370 tons. As it happened, the small Atlantic and 4-4-0 No 59 had the heaviest trains. All the advance portions carried 'Train Following' red-painted boards on the rear of the last coach. This, and/or extra tail lamp applied for the return journey due into Kings Cross soon after 22.00. On that night in 1913 there were delays and congestion after a fine, hot weekend, with a number of extra main line semi-fasts and outer suburban trains. The last Skegness did not pass Wood Green until after 23.30 when the approaches to the terminus were probably still rather bunged up.

London engines and men worked throughout on the Skegness trains, as they did mostly with Atlantics on the Sunday half-day 'Provinces' excursions (advertised to start at 11.35) to Retford and Grimsby and back. These offered bookings to Peterborough and principal stations beyond at fares around 4s 6d (22½p) — 6s 6d (32½p), also through portions to Nottingham and Lincoln on certain dates, all involving about 12hr duty for the crews with a break at destination. In the height of summer Sundays the Skegness in two portions and the 'Provinces' in three or occasionally four, got mixed up together in close succession with the 11.40 ordinary express to York; the 11.50 to Cambridge and the 12.00 to Leeds. After that, apart from a slow and suburban train there was only the heavy 17.10 for Hitchin, Peterborough, and principal stations to Leeds, York and NER until the night Scottish expresses. Sunday main line services were very thin ordinarily with no day Anglo-Scottish trains. For many years there was a suburban 'Churchtime Interval' with no services between about 10.45 and 13.00.

The story of the Yarmouth Beach M&GN excursions makes for rather amazing reading. Sponsored by the Sons of Phoenix Friendly Society whose rather impecunious-looking representatives wearing blue sashes sold tickets outside Kings Cross local station, on certain dates in the holiday season their trains provided very cheap (though far from luxurious) travel with 1 (midnight start), 2, 3, or 8-day bookings. The Society advertised on flimsy handbills fixed to billboards and shop windows, also at some London area stations. The stock was old suburban sets and six-wheelers for a slow, roundabout 187-mile journey via Peterborough and South Lynn. Starting times were 09.10 on Friday or Saturday; Saturday midnight and, sometimes 15.45, and Sunday morning at 08.30.

After calling at some suburban stations, the trains were then fast to Peterborough and hauled by odd engines stationed there: sometimes Singles, more generally 4-4-0s. There were return trains late on a Sunday night, but mainly these came up on a Friday evening when the period passengers moved in bulk. On

Below: Ivatt small Atlantic, or 'Klondyke', No 257 on a Manchester-Kings Cross express at Potters Bar. *LPC*

15 August 1913, five specials were run, all headed by Peterborough 4-4-0s. Three each consisted of two 11-coach suburban sets. One had a similar four-wheeled set and a string of old six-wheelers including a close-coupled 'three' as used for provincial workmen's trains. The other train comprised sixteen teak M&GN six-wheelers which had to be returned empty at once, as did some of the other rakes required for further weekend excursion use. These lengthy outfits may have presented problems at some passing places on the Joint Line which provided all the locomotives east of Peterborough.

Special trains of many kinds were fairly numerous. Some of these with dining cars and first-class accommodation were provided for race meetings, or for liner sailings from Hull, Immingham or Tyne Dock. Others were for party and public excursions. There were many livestock or equipment trains operated in connection with horse, cattle and flower shows and the like. Neither must one forget military or other services' movements, emigrants' trains; special workings via the Met widened lines and many others.

A long-disappeared and considerable milk traffic in churns came to London from the GN and North Staffordshire Railway country stations on the Stafford-Uttoxeter-Derby (Friargate) route. It was sufficient to require two trains each weekday night, joining the main line at Grantham from Colwick (Nottingham). The first of these ran non-stop between Grantham and Finsbury Park hauled by the Kings Cross Atlantic off the 17.30 down express. The second train made one or two main line calls, being worked by a Grantham 4-4-0 or small 4-4-2 which went back with the 06.30 milk empties. The other empties went down soon after midday, being an odd locomotive turn for some time. In both directions long stops were made at Finsbury Park for loading, unloading, transferring to and from road and suburban railway vans, all of which created a frightful clatter!

On a busy FA Cup-Final Saturday I was often up at dawn to watch and note down thirty or more inward overnight and early morning excursion specials with their numerous six-wheeled and other saloons. The stock could include the varied liveries, ancient and more modern styles, belonging to the NE, GC, Cheshire Lines, North Staffordshire, L&Y, M&GN, and possibly others, but until after grouping all such trains were handled by GN engines.

There was the astonishing appearance on 1 August 1914 of NE 3-cyl 4-4-2 No 2170 on a York-Kings Cross period excursion, returning with a similar one in the afternoon and formed of small coaches fitted only

Below: The famous '3.40pm' 'Scotsman' fast goods climbing Potters Bar bank headed by Gresley 2-cyl 'Ragtime' 2-6-0 No 1674. *Rixon Bucknall Collection/Ian Allan Library*

Above: Gresley 2-cyl 2-8-0 No 475 at Hornsey shed.
H. Gordon Tidey

with Westinghouse brake. The Atlantic was the only NE locomotive south of Doncaster I saw or heard of for certain until the 1920s, at any rate in the London area. *Recent research suggests that two or three NER locomotives made their appearance in the 1900s (Ed)*

Arriving at Wood Green homeward bound one December Saturday in 1913, I was told that the signalman from the up south box had a message for me. It was to let me know that he had heard on the 'Needle' (telegraph instrument) that an enormous new engine had left Peterborough with a coal train. I went down to Hatfield after lunch and luckily secured a good view, including its footplate and the huge-looking firebox interior. This was No 456, the pioneer Gresley 2-cyl 2-8-0. With its sisters this was soon to take regular 80-wagon mineral loads, and led to the large stud of 3-cyl and more powerful examples fitted with the conjugated valve gear actuating the inside motion.

A notable sight in 1914, passing as light engines singly or in pairs, were the fifteen 2-4-0s fitted with domed boilers going on loan to the SE&CR mostly from the provinces. Some had never been seen in London before. With chimneys removed they travelled via the Met Widened Lines, hauled presumably to Bricklayers' Arms. Their numbers were: 204/6, 699, 714, 756/9, 820, 895/8, 991/2/4/5, 1067/9.

For some years I kept a continuous record of the train mileages run by the large Atlantics stationed at Kings Cross. All the regular workings were on an out-and-home basis and almost invariably with one crew. Having the privilege of access to the working notices of special trains and being closely in touch with daily happenings, I was nearly always able to settle any queries by intuition or with the help of friendly railwaymen. Each of the first and second link drivers had his 'own' engine which, whenever possible, he took on slower and secondary duties as well as the longer principal ones. At busy periods, though, and at times of locomotive shortages, the Atlantics had to be sent out with other crews as well.

Counted from Sunday morning to Saturday night, Atlantic mileage totals topping the lists in peak August weeks of 1913 were as follows:

Table 2

First week	Second week	Third week
No 1426, 2,090 miles	No 1444, 2,228 miles	No 301, 2,048 miles
No 1461, 2,007 miles	No 278, 2,152 miles	No 278, 1,790 miles
No 1444, 1,986 miles	No 1440, 2,095 miles	No 1444, 1,787 miles

Over quarterly periods including quieter times, short spells in shed for maintenance or examination, and days standing pilot, typically good averages were around 1,250-1,350 miles per week. There was a particularly fine achievement by No 1460 of the 1910 superheated, modified series with a total of 81,578 miles in 65 weeks when going to Plant Works. Nos 299 and 1400 ran 80,882 miles in 78 weeks, and 88,482 in 85 weeks respectively. The Atlantics sometimes ran over 100,000 miles between shoppings, as did the Pacifics a good many years after, though these usually accumulated their miles more quickly under much more arduous running conditions. Overhaul, general or intermediate repair, part replacement work and the like at Doncaster, or in shed workshops, was a lengthy business. There were no moving belts or time and work studies then!

On the question of fares, there were no regular cheap day return tickets but the third-class single fare was only 1d a mile, with a slight reduction for many of the returns in the suburban area and second-class at a few pence more. Day excursions, often by special trains, were offered for all sorts of events, and there were some day or half-day tickets with a late night return from provincial towns to London. But there was hardly anything to or from the NER or Scotland, other than holiday period excursions, and, of course, tourist and weekend tickets.

Towards the end of July and during the first days of August 1914, long-distance holiday traffic was probably at its pre-grouping peak, but we were on the brink of a precipice! Behind the scenes in certain shipping and railway régimes I knew that large vessels were being requisitioned for conversion to hospital ships and armed merchant cruisers; special trains were ordered to convey reservists and Territorials returned home from camp pending general mobilisation. The next decade of the Great Northern was a mixed story, but one thing was certain, those railway heydays before 1914 had gone for ever.

Below: No 2 speed express goods at Wood Green behind Gresley superheated 0-6-0 No 73. *LPC*

Winter on the 'Long Drag'

STEPHEN McGAHON

Above: 15 February 1979: Train No 8G80 gets under way from Appleby, after being shunted for train No 1M70, the 09.35 Carlisle-Nottingham, to precede. *P. A. Holden*

Bad weather has always played a major part in the working of the Settle-Carlisle line and the winter of 1979 wrote another memorable chapter in its history, causing considerable operating difficulties and creating scenes reminiscent of previous harsh winters with snow-filled cuttings and trains often in trouble on the long climbs. As a signalman on the line I was able to experience these events at first-hand and gain an inside view of the struggle to keep open England's highest main line.

On several occasions between December 1978 and the following April, Carlisle's snowploughs were called upon to clear the line, but by far the most eventful period was the week beginning Monday, 12 February when there began what turned out to be a week of continuous work on the line south of Appleby.

Heavy snow fell during the Monday and Tuesday of that week on the higher stretches of the line, although there were few delays at the time. By Wednesday morning, however, the blizzards had reached the lowlands and as I reported for duty at 22.00, I was joined by platelayers Les Egglestone and Dickie Birtle.

Working 12-hour shifts in their capacity of 'snowmen', they would have the job of keeping signals and points and, in our case, the level crossing free of snow. They had been called out by my colleague Jimmy Richardson earlier that evening when it was clear that the weather was deteriorating; no doubt at such places as Garsdale and Blea Moor, 'snowmen' would have been on duty since Monday.

On Wednesday afternoon the Carlisle snowplough had been joined by another, this time from Lostock Hall, Preston. These two worked between Kirkby Stephen and Garsdale and Garsdale and Blea Moor respectively until that night when strengthening winds began to cause heavy drifting. More immediately, the crossover road at Garsdale was being filled in as fast as it could be dug out, eventually forcing the snowploughs to run all the way between Kirkby Stephen and Blea Moor before crossing over — a distance of 18 miles. Their slow speed combined with the long distances the ploughs had to run in front of trains began to cause delays to the scheduled services,

79

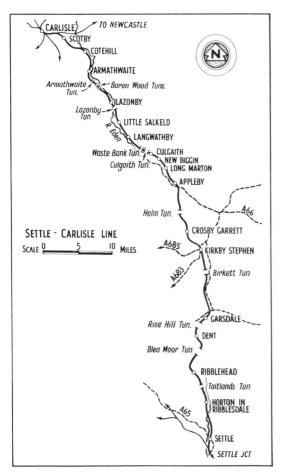

SETTLE - CARLISLE LINE
SCALE 0 5 10 MILES

particularly on the up line, where a block signalling failure resulted in all trains being stopped at Kirkby Stephen and cautioned into the section to Garsdale. This was an added handicap for heavy trains on the climb to Ais Gill and was to become significant the next morning.

When dawn came on Thursday, there were trains standing on the up line at every signalbox from Blea Moor to Long Meg. The storms were worsening as two down trains became stuck for a short time on the single line between Blea Moor and Horton in Ribblesdale, and although they managed to struggle through and continue their journeys, this greatly extended the delays to up trains. This was best illustrated by train No 8G80, the 06.00 Carlisle to Bescot goods, which arrived at Culgaith at 06.38, was still present when I was relieved by my colleague Charlie Rae, at 07.10, and eventually left at 09.00.

The backlog of up trains cleared just in time for what proved to be the main event of the day, and, indeed, the week, involving 7A09, the 09.34 Carlisle-Willesden goods, a 1,000-ton train hauled by Class 40 1-Co-Co-1 No 40.132. Incidentally, emergency arrangements say that in such conditions train loads should be reduced by up to 50%. After the caution at Kirkby Stephen, 7A09 faced a continuous struggle, and in "white-out" conditions was reduced to walking pace by the time it approached Ais Gill summit. Stopping at Ais Gill box the driver phoned for assistance but on returning to his train found it had

Below: 15 February: Appleby Traffic Assistant, Norman Greenhow, advises the driver of 1M70 09.35 Carlisle-Nottingham of conditions further south. *P. A. Holden*

Right: 16 February: The ice-encrusted 25.172 on snowplough duty at Blea Moor. *Author*

become hemmed in by drifts and could move neither forward nor back. With no immediate chance of receiving assistance, the only thing to do was to abandon the train, and so the snowplough was summoned to rescue the train crew, a task which almost saw the snowplough becoming stuck as well. The following train, No 6E01, the Carlisle-Healey Mills freight, was accordingly shunted into Kirkby's up refuge siding and the locomotive returned to Carlisle. From then on, all up trains were diverted or cancelled although, for some reason, the 16.10 Glasgow-Nottingham express passenger was allowed to proceed as far as Appleby before being turned back to Carlisle and then diverted via the West Coast and Carnforth to Leeds lines.

The stranded 7A09 quickly became buried and by the night was trapped by roof-high drifts on one side and, on the other, by packed snow ploughed from the down line. That same evening, the Thursday, a party of children who had been camping(!) in Dentdale were picked up from Dent station and taken to Skipton by the Lostock Hall snowplough. A sad note was struck with the news that two platelayers involved in snow duties at Hellifield had been killed by the late running Nottingham-Glasgow express.

Thursday's night shift passed off comparatively uneventfully, with the traffic inspectors first considering, and then dismissing, the possibility of introducing single-line working between Kirkby Stephen and Blea Moor. Their decision was reached because of the length of section involved, taking into account the already singled section beyond Blea Moor to Horton in Ribblesdale due to work on Ribblehead Viaduct. As I signed off on Friday morning, the snow had stopped and the last of Thursday's down trains was passing. By then, I decided to forego the pleasure of sleep and see for myself the cause of all the problems further up the line. I hitched a ride to Appleby on the engineers' ballast locomotive with Inspector Calder who was to be that day's traffic department representative on the snowplough. He described the previous day's conditions at Ais Gill as the worst he had encountered in nearly 50 years on the railway.

For the whole of that week Appleby had acted as a base for the two different Carlisle snowploughs used; each consisted of pairs of Class 25 Bo-Bo locomotives

Left: 16 February: Nos 25.172/285 with the Carlisle snowplough stand on the crossover at Blea Moor, after running wrong line from Kirkby Stephen. *Author*

Top right: 15 February: Train No 7E84, the 07.30 Carlisle-Tinsley freight at Appleby, having been put inside for the 09.35 Carlisle-Nottingham, leaves the sidings while the ill-fated train No 7A09 waits on the main line. *P. A. Holden*

Right: 17 February: At Ais Gill the rescue train behind a Class 47 has arrived and the mechanical digger has been unloaded. *P. A. Holden*

with a plough unit at each end. As most of their work was south of Appleby, they returned to Carlisle only for refuelling, crew changeovers being effected by the use of light engines. The latter were often locomotives unfit for hauling a train. The light engines came from Carlisle about every four hours; this gave each loco crew and the two fitters (there in case of loco problems), an eight-hour shift including travelling time to and from Appleby. However, the rest of the staff of traffic, permanent and motive power inspectors often worked up to 12 hours.

For my ride to Appleby I chose the rear cab of Class 25 No 25.172 which, with 25.285, had been on this duty since 18.00 on Wednesday. We left Appleby under a clear sky with the sun shining. Also in the cab were two platelayers travelling to Kirkby Stephen: on occasions such as this the snowplough tended to be used as an unofficial bus service ferrying platelayers and signalmen to their place of duty. This practice was a cause of frustration to signalmen and controllers because of the long times spent in section, leading to delays to following trains. But there was no chance of this happening on my trip as we were the only train moving in the 43 miles between Appleby and Settle Junction. As far as Kirkby Stephen there was little snow on the lines but here the railway begins to climb more steeply into the Pennines up to the 1,169 feet

high Ais Gill summit. Now Inspector Calder took possession of the line to allow us to travel wrong road to Blea Moor and it became a matter of almost continuous ploughing during which a curtain of snow was thrown past the cab window and on to the up line, now invisible for most of way southwards. As we slowed at Ais Gill the stricken 7A09 Carlisle-Willesden freight could be seen almost completely buried on the eastern side. The rest of the cutting was at least 5-6ft deep as I could touch snow simply by putting a hand out of the cab window. The up starting signal arm remained in the off position, encased in a foot-thick block of frozen snow. A stop at Garsdale gave me a chance to get out and take some photographs, but not until I had cleared away a solid wall of snow which had filled the doorway. It was difficult to get the door closed again and unless I had done so the rest of the journey would have been spent with the cab filling up with snow thrown up by the plough.

From Garsdale we literally ploughed on towards Dent where the famous snow fences above the station seemed to have had little effect on the formation of an enormous drift. This had obliterated all signs of the up side platform and shelter and the up line, leaving only the top 4ft of the up home signal visible. The bright sunshine served to emphasise Dentdale's picturesqueness and inaccessibility, for we could see the deep drifts on the road into the dale under Dent Head viaduct, just before we plunged into the depths of Blea Moor Tunnel. At the far end of the tunnel, we paused to drop off some trackwalkers, a job few would relish in such weather, particularly after noting the hundreds of fearsome icicles hanging from the tunnel roof.

The furthest point of our journey was reached at the beleaguered outpost of Blea Moor, a study in isolation with its deserted railway cottages and water tower huddled around the wind-battered and snow-covered signalbox. Access was possible only by rail, and even with a bright sun and blue sky overhead, visibility was less than 200 yards, thanks to the constant haze of drifting snow. In their 40 hours of continuous use, the locomotives had become thickly encrusted with ice, particularly on their roofs and leading ends.

On hearing that the Lostock Hall snowplough was on its way and would follow us down to Kirkby Stephen, we departed northwards from the white emptiness of Blea Moor. Before long, we had a demonstration of how quickly the line can become blocked for the plough was shifting as much snow as it

Top left: 17 February: The scene at Ais Gill. *P. A. Holden*

Left: 17 February: Platelayers dig out the wagons of the snowbound train No 7A09 while the mechanical digger clears a path to the rear of the train. *P. A. Holden*

Top right: 17 February: At Ais Gill, rescue is at hand for locomotive No 40.132. *P. A. Holden*

had on the outward journey. The windows of the leading cab of the locomotive I was riding on suffered a constant battering from the avalanche of snow thrown up by the plough and over the roof of the leading locomotive — a very spectacular sight.

The sole beneficiary of that morning's work by two sets of snowploughs was train No 6S78, the 22.45 Llandeilo to Mossend air-braked Speedlink freight, and in the event this was the last scheduled train to use the line until the Sunday evening.

Our arrival back at Appleby at about 12.30 meant another change of crew and I returned to Culgaith on the returning relief engine. After snatching a few hours sleep I reported back to the box for a Friday night shift devoid of trains, apart from relief engines.

As not much snow had fallen since Friday morning, and forecasts indicated an improvement in the weather, the operation to free train No 7A09 and reopen the line began in earnest early on Saturday. The first train up from Carlisle consisted of a Class 47 locomotive hauling three coaches, a number of empty spoil wagons, and a Lowmac wagon with a mechanical digger aboard. Having collected a small army of platelayers at Appleby, the train then proceeded to Kirkby Stephen, crossed to the down line and went forward to Ais Gill to stand just short of 7A09 and here the mechanical digger was unloaded. Meanwhile, the snowplough had followed in on the up line and approached as close as possible to the rear of the stranded train. The last few feet were left to be removed by the digger, and the gangs of platelayers cleared packed snow by hand from between the wheels and couplings of the rear half of the train. The snowplough then retreated, to be replaced by a pair of Class 40 locomotives which hauled the liberated

wagons down to Kirkby Stephen. A repeat performance with the remainder of the train saw the two halves of 7A09 reunited at Kirkby Stephen, to return northwards to Carlisle. Although basically simple the whole operation was laborious in its execution, taking the best part of nine hours to complete.

With the major obstruction removed, it now remained to clear the up line of substantial amounts of snow that had accumulated during the previous three days. An all-out effort was made on the Sunday morning using snowploughs, mechanical plant and gangs of men. At Dent, the worst affected spot, soldiers were brought in to dig out the enormous drifts which had enveloped the station. By early evening the job had been finished and the line was reopened to scheduled traffic with train No 1M87, the 15.15 Glasgow-Nottingham express passenger. Carlisle snowplough stayed on duty through Sunday night and Monday, returning home on Monday evening. By then, traffic had returned to normal and a thaw had set in. So ended seven days which are bound to remain long in the memories of those involved. For me, they brought to life events which previously I had only glimpsed second-hand through books and photographs.

The services of the ploughs were called upon several more times before the end of 1979's winter, but at no time were trains so badly disrupted as in mid-February.

My thanks are due to my signalman colleague at Appleby, Paul Holden, for help in preparing this account. I think it is appropriate to dedicate it to all railwaymen who at all hours and in all weathers, endeavour, for an often unappreciative public, to keep lines open and trains running.

A steam Sapper's saga

R. M. TYRRELL

At the outbreak of World War 2 I tried to join the Royal Engineers Transportation Department but was told: 'Sorry, no vacancies.' The next best thing to a steam locomotive seemed to be a tank, so I joined the Royal Tank Regiment instead and spent the next five years in armour in several very hot and dusty countries.

On repatriation in late 1945 I felt I had had enough of the stink of petrol, diesel and cordite fumes and I longed for a fresh breath of steam. Accordingly, I again applied to be a 'Railway Sapper'. Now, it seemed there was a shortage of that species and I was accepted at once. I still had a year to do.

I was posted to Longmoor Transportation Training Centre, then the Mecca of military railwaymen, for an 'Officers' Refresher Course'. I certainly needed some refreshing, for before the war I had only been a Premium Apprentice on the Southern, the lowest form of animal-life in any railway hierarchy.

The course was in two parts, theory and practice. Theory was mainly concerned with safety — braking systems and signalling in particular.

Army railway practice, I soon learned, differed quite a bit from the civilian. For example, a signalman was called a blockman because the former term might be confused with a private soldier in the Royal Corps of Signals. An allegedly true story circulated at Longmoor about a raw recruit who, on giving his civilian occupation as a 'blockman' was immediately assigned to a signalbox where he was expected to know how to pull off 1,000-yard 'distants'. It turned out that the poor man had been a butcher's blockman, an assistant used to hacking up meat carcasses on the wooden block.

Again, it was mandatory soon after leaving a station, for the fireman to lean out of the cab, look back at his train and report to the driver: 'Train complete!' Presumably this was just in case some Gremlin (transferred from the RAF) had uncoupled the last few vehicles and put the brake-pipe back on the plug!

The practical side of my course was sheer joy: locomotive preparation, firing, driving, disposal and maintenance. My sergeant instructors were mostly regular railwaymen, signed on for the duration, with plenty of overseas service and experience. They liked a little joke, too. For instance, near Woolmer there was a road overbridge from which some nasty little boys tried to drop stones down a locomotive's chimney as it passed. But the sergeants had the answer to that trick — just as the engine reached the bridge a shovelful of sand was shot into the firebox and the regulator slammed wide open. A stream of soot sprayed out of the chimney and the little dears ran home to their mothers with faces black as crows! The instructors would wink and say: 'Anyway, sir, that cleans the tubes much better than they do it on shed.'

Apart from carrying War Department freight and stores the Longmoor Military Railway ran a scheduled passenger service which connected with the Southern Railway main lines at Liss and Borden respectively, so although Longmoor was in the middle of nowhere it was not really isolated.

The locomotive stud at that time was very varied. Naturally, the 'Austerity' 2-10-0s and 2-8-0s predominated along with the 0-6-0 tanks but there were also several venerable tank engines some dating, I think, from the days of the original Woolmer Instructional Military Railway, as the LMR was once called. There was, too, an oil-fired ex-GWR 'Dean Goods' 0-6-0 which regularly caught fire and had to be doused by the Army Fire Service.

Finally, we had two ex-LB&SCR Atlantic tanks which somehow seemed very incongruous on this line and it was on one of these (to use a mixed metaphor) that I nearly met my Waterloo. By the time my course was nearing its end and with the expert help of my instructors (Staff-Sergeants Skingle and Smith) my driving and firing had become reasonably competent. But one day as we drew up at Liss station the former remarked, quite casually: 'Smudger and me are just popping over to the local for a pint. Would you mind

Left: A latter-day view of the now-closed depot and workshops of the Longmoor Military Railway. *Bryan H. Kimber*

cleaning the fire, sir? You've got exactly twenty minutes.'

So this was to be my acid test! It suddenly dawned on me that these NCOs rightly considered that an officer who couldn't clean a fire had no right to the respect of his men and a young captain who had come from 'some tank outfit' was particularly suspect. Moreover, up till then I had never cleaned a fire on anything bigger than the 15-inch gauge.

I set to work with a will. Although it was late December, in five minutes I stripped to shirt-sleeve order. I attacked that fire alternately with the pricker, the dart and the clinker-shovel.

Each in turn contracted 'brewer's droop' as it got red-hot and had to be withdrawn to cool off. Also, as any real fireman knows, it is an even harder task to clean the fire on a tank engine than a tender one because there is limited space and the handles of the fire-irons have a nasty tendency to poke out the rear cab windows. I was literally dripping with sweat as my two sergeants sauntered back from the boozer, climbed up and surveyed the footplate and the firebox.

Goodness knows how, I had managed to achieve a clean fire, full pressure and half-a-glass of water. Staff-Sergeant Smith slowly lit a Woodbine and as he exhaled the smoke, remarked: 'You'll do, sir.' I could not have wished for any higher praise!

That night I celebrated my 'passing-out' (perhaps in more senses than one) at the Royal Anchor Hotel in Liphook, a well-known venue, and one made all the more attractive because the then owner (the late Charlie Lane) had a $10\frac{1}{4}$in gauge line in the garden and a remarkable collection of model locomotives of all sizes.

Nobody who served at Longmoor at that time could forget its commandant. He rejoiced to the singularly un-English name of Joly de-la-Lotbinière. Despite this he was the prototype of the best kind of English gentleman. Any young officer in difficulties could go to 'Joly's' office for advice. The old boy would get up from his desk, come round and put his hand on one's shoulder and say: 'Never mind, me boy - we'll sort it out somehow.' We all devoutly wished that more senior army officers could have been such an ideal father-figure.

In the last days of 1945 I was due to be posted to BAOR. I was genuinely sad to leave Longmoor; it was such a civilised place, with a modern officers' mess, the luxury of hot baths and good English cooking, served by pretty ATS girls — such a contrast to the dusty deserts and insect-ridden jungles of my previous experience.

Of my journey to join No 164 Railway Operating Company RE I remember very little except the intense cold. On New Year's Eve 1945/46 I crossed from Harwich to The Hook of Holland and entered a freez-

Above: Not a railway disaster, but a simulated accident for a re-railing exercise on the LMR during the writer's training, featuring Dean Goods 0-6-0 WD No 70195. *Author*

Below: WD 0-6-0T No 010 *Woolmer*, on Longmoor shed on 2 June 1954.

Bottom: The ex-Shropshire and Montgomeryshire Rly 0-4-2 *Gazelle* when displayed on the main square at Longmoor Camp, seen in June 1953. *Both: R. E. Vincent*

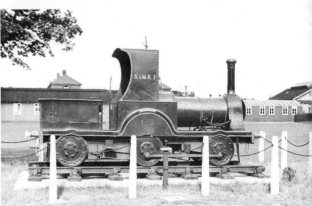

Above: A surprising overnight visitor to Krefeld shed was this German-built 4-6-0, destined for the Norwegian State Railways, a delivery long-delayed by the war.

Left: The writer on the footplate of WD 'Austerity' 2-10-0 No 73663, on shed at Hohenbudberg, Krefeld. *Both: Author*

ing train. Due to a shortage of steam heat connections my compartment resembled a refrigerator and there was actually ice on the inside of the windows.

Luckily, on the advice of the old Longmoor hands, I had armed myself with a hip-flask of rum and I was desperately grateful for it. What I didn't drink I smeared on the windows with my handkerchief to get some kind of view of Germany. As the next day dawned I peered through the glass and saw the havoc wrought by the RAF and the USAF in the Ruhr. Whole towns and villages had simply disappeared and grey-faced citizens wandered around aimlessly in a dazed manner searching for something that they couldn't even remember.

On arrival at my unit I was surprised but pleased to be told that I was to be sent on detachment to take charge of a running shed just outside Krefeld, not far from Cologne. Luckily this depot had escaped the bombing and was intact. It housed about fifty locomotives, mostly British 'Austerities' with a sprinkling of German Class 50 2-10-0 'Kriegsloks'. The main task of my little sub-unit was to instruct the German footplate crews in handling the 'Austerities' which had been sent out to ease the desperate shortage of German motive power.

The bulk of the traffic was coal and freight for it was vital to get the German economy on the rails again, but our engines also had another important task — the army leave trains to the coast via Holland. This link was always crewed by my own Sappers, including (whenever possible) myself!

I was exceptionally lucky in having three superb sergeants to support me. There was one in charge of each eight-hour shift. All of them were railwaymen in civilian life and without them we would scarcely have turned a wheel. This just confirmed an opinion, long held during my service with the Royal Tank Regiment, that sergeants are the backbone of the armed forces.

The loco shed was modern and well-equipped and the shedmaster's office was impressive by British standards. I formed an impression there, often later confirmed, that in Europe railwaymen enjoy a far higher niche in the social scale than they do in Britain. I have often pondered why this should be so . . .

I sat (as seldom as possible) at a huge desk, opposite Herr Schmidt, the real 'Guvnor', flanked by four telephones. At a smaller table were the shift-sergeant and an efficient young German interpreter named Leopold. He was kept on his toes for my German language was minimal and he couldn't possibly be everywhere at once.

Nevertheless, it is a great tribute to the ordinary Sappers that they contrived so successfully to train the German footplate men to operate our 'Austerities' — 'those simple little locomotives', as one German driver described them.

Relations between the German staff and ourselves were good but there was one minor mystery I never solved — the frequent theft of locomotive headlamps. Time and again footplatemen returned from a trip without them and could offer no explanation. As this was long before the time that lamps had any value on the 'gricer' market I simply don't know where they went. I can only surmise that even these humble accessories had their price on the flourishing black market, like almost everything else.

Perhaps, more than any other railwayman, a shedmaster is faced with sudden emergencies and unexpected problems. For example, very early one morning I was roused out of my bed by the shift-sergeant who said: 'There is a slight dreariness on shed, I'm sorry to tell you, air.' Arriving on the scene I saw the tender of a Class 50 'Kriegslok' sitting in the well of the turntable.

Above: WD 'Austerity' 2-10-0 No 73755 at Calais on 9 May 1945; this locomotive is now preserved at the Dutch State Railways museum at Utrecht. *Dutch Railway Museum*

Apparently the German driver had failed to notice that the table was not set for his road and he had failed to make an emergency Westinghouse application before it was too late. With the turntable *hors de combat* we couldn't get our steam crane on duty and nobody, not even my excellent sergeants, seemed to know what to do. I was foxed, too.

Then, I suddenly recalled a practical Tank Regiment exercise called 'Unditching and Towing'. Accordingly, I gave orders for a 2-10-0 'Austerity' (which was spare in steam) to come round to the front of the troubled Class 50 and couple up. With liberal application of sand, full-gear and a slamming open of the regulator, we got the tender back on the road.

According to 'King's' Regulations' — the army officers' Bible — an officer's first duty is the welfare of his men. Soldiers have not (yet) any union to protect them so they must rely on their officers in emergencies. One day a Sapper requested a personal interview with me. He complained:

'Sir, a German kitchen-maid in our mess threatened to murder me with a butcher's knife.' I had take the threat seriously as I had been warned that there could be some neo-Nazis in the area and, if I found any, I must report them to the authorities. However, after a session with the two parties and my faithful interpreter, Leopold, it turned out that my Sapper had made what police courts *used* to call 'an improper suggestion' to the maiden. She wasn't having any and I advised the Sapper to seek his leisure elsewhere.

I was in luck, as regards my living quarters. I was billeted in the house of a retired German loco driver and his wife. It was modern, light and airy — a complete contrast to the Victorian, dingy dwellings in Ashford's SE&CR railway town where I had spent my apprenticeship. Again, this gave me the impression that, although Britain is the 'Father of the Railway', she has somehow lamentably failed to give her railwaymen the 'status' that they have richly deserved.

Many people in their sixties will remember that the winter of 1945/46 was a swine. It was hellish cold and many people had real problems to survive. But not my Sappers and me! No. With unlimited loco coal from the shed, we never spent a warmer postwar winter!

Nevertheless, leisure time was a problem, for both my men and myself. ENSA shows and YMCA reading rooms had not had a chance to get organised in our area at that time and the dull evenings nearly got me court-martialled. An UNRRA officer, who shared the Pioneer Corps mess where I fed, invited me to a German cabaret show in Krefeld. It was an excellent evening, with everything perfectly decent but (unknown to both of us) it took place in an out-of-bounds brothel area.

Just as we were leaving, the place was raided by the Military Police and my name was taken. A week later I was marched in front of the Area Commander, a Brigadier. My own OC, the well-loved Major Bray, did everything he could to help but warned me I might be court-martialled for this unwitting, technical offence.

But three lucky things got me off: the Brigadier weighed my reasonable war-record, I was able to tell him that the Military Police sergeant who took my name was chewing gum on duty and the Brigadier (I heard later) had just won £100 on a horse race. These events had put him in a good mood and I was released with a friendly lecture.

Talking of disciplinary matters, I must mention the most remarkable of my three efficient sergeants: he was Jock McCulloch, a man from the northern reaches of the LNER. Whenever I was faced with a disciplinary problem (which was seldom) I learnt to hand it over to this braw Scot. He had just one formula: 'Leave it to me, sir, I'll smash his chest in!' I never did discover just how Jock fixed his victims — I just know that they never transgressed a second time and he never lost his popularity.

The WD 'Austerities' were on the whole trouble-free and efficient engines and although they looked incongruous heading a rake of SE&CR 'birdcage' stock against the Ruhr countryside on the leave-trains, they must have given our troops a pleasant reminder of 'Blighty' for which they were homeward-bound.

The 'Austerities' had one peculiar fault. Due to some mis-design of the drawgear between engine and tender, at a critical speed of about 35mile/h an unpleasant fore-and-aft motion began. The sergeants called it 'rogering' and when I took the regulator I was warned not to exceed this speed, especially by Staff-Sergeant Terry, a very careful engineman who, by a happy coincidence, came from Ashford shed on the Southern Railway.

'Look, Staff,' I said one day. 'You say that 35mile/h is this critical speed. Right, if we exceed it then it won't be critical any longer?' 'OK, sir, have a go if you like — I'll hang on to the handrail, but don't blame me if we finish up in a cornfield!' So I eased the lever a bit further across the quadrant and, after a few shivers, our 2-10-0 was running as sweet as a sewing machine and we were swinging along at a good 50. We reached our Dutch destination some 20 mins early, much to the delight of the troops going on leave.

All too soon, my demobilisation day was looming up. I would be sorry to leave Germany where I had been doing a useful job, as opposed to killing my fellow human beings, which I had been engaged in for the previous six years.

When my personal 'D-Day' came I was given a whale of a send-off party by my loyal sergeants and men. Next morning, assisted by their strong arms I sadly staggered aboard the leave train that I had so often driven.

Alas, the Longmoor Military Railway is now no more. I went to its funeral in company with brother steam Sappers and it was a sad day. More recently, in early 1978 I made a last sentimental journey to Longmoor. That really wrung the heartstrings.

Gone are the loco shed and the workshops, and the Continental-type signalbox at Longmoor Downs has been bulldozed to the ground. There are now only two remaining memorials to this once-great military railway training centre where generations of Britons learnt how to operate lines all over the world.

One is *Gazelle*, Britain's smallest-ever standard-gauge locomotive, ex-Shropshire and Montgomeryshire Railway. She stood rusting outside the former HQ block where dear Brigadier 'Joly' used to encourage his young officers and men, until she was rescued for preservation at the National Railway Museum. Secondly, a few pathetic feet of rail still remain in the tarmac road from Liphook where innumerable train guards used to dismount and flag the train across.

No more will the 'Sappers' Song' be heard, nor will the wail of an 'Austerity's' whistle again echo through the Hampshire woods. The LMR has finished and a great chapter of military railway history has closed. The War Office, with its infallible (?) judgement has decided that in the next conflict, mountains of men, munitions and materials can be moved better by a fleet of lorries than by a railway system. Are they right? Those who survive will see.

LT & S steam interlude

In recent years the former London, Tilbury and Southend Railway lines have seldom featured in railway publications, probably because the present-day 25kV ac electric multiple-unit trains are held to have little interest. From the end of World War II up to electrification of the main passenger services in 1962, the LT&S was of considerable interest. The line's varying spheres of control in the past, latterly in the hands of the LMS, were given a further twist with the transfer of the Tilbury section to the Eastern Region on 20 February 1949. The former LT&SR and LMS motive power was complemented by Austerity, BR, and ex-LNER types and LNER and BR rolling stock was introduced. These pages show a little of the variety in BR days.

Above: At Campbell Road Junction, Bow, the LT&SR proper was joined by the Metropolitan District Railway from Whitechapel; this connection was taken out before electrification of the LT&S. Here BR '4' 2-6-4T No 80072 approaches the junction with a train out of Fenchurch St on 18 May 1959. *Frank Church*

Below: The LT&S 4-4-2Ts and LMS-built examples were relegated to secondary work by the early 1950s. LMS-built No 41944 heads a Pitsea-Tilbury train near Mucking in 1953. *P. Ransome-Wallis*

Left: The LT&S 0-6-2Ts remained at work until the late 1950s. Here Nos 41985/86 double-head oil tank empties near Dagenham Dock in July 1952. *P. Ransome-Wallis*

Centre left: The Stanier 3-cyl 2-6-4Ts were an LT&S section speciality and performed nobly. No 42512 proceeds under newly installed wires with the 10.32 ex-Fenchurch St on August Bank Holiday 1960. The first eight vehicles of its train were a special, largely BR, non-corridor set normally used for the 16.00 'Flyer' ex-London. *P. I. Paton*

Below: Twilight for steam: four 2-6-4Ts made redundant by LT&S electrification make their way from Shoeburyness depot to new homes, on 8 July 1962. Seen at Thorpe Bay are Fairburn 2-6-4Ts Nos 42227/218/226 and BR '4' No 80071.
M. Edwards

Top right: LNER-design non-corridor stock forms part of 3-cyl 2-6-4T No 42514's train, as it enters Pitsea with the 11.10 Shoeburyness-Fenchurch St on 3 November 1961.
M. Edwards

Centre right: Boat trains from St Pancras-Tilbury Docks gave added interest. 'Crab' 2-6-0 No 42839 approaches Tilbury with one such working on 8 July 1950. *H. C. Casserley*

Bottom right: There were through trains from elsewhere, too, such as this Whit Sunday 1961 excursion from Hinckley-Southend Central nearing its goal behind Fairburn 2-6-4T No 42237. *M. Edwards*

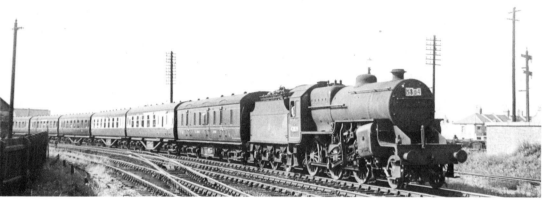

The Portuguese metre gauge

SAM LAMBERT

All photographs by Sam Lambert, May 1979

If you require a starting point for my visit to the railways of north Portugal it would be *Narrow Gauge the World Over* by Whitehouse and Allen (pub Ian Allan) which was a Christmas present from my wife and not a total surprise, I may add. This book of charming memories set me thinking. Was there anywhere in Western Europe where a narrow gauge system might survive with steam-hauled trains — other than as a very obvious tourist attraction? It seemed to me that the Iberian peninsula offered the best bet and Portugal with its six metre gauge lines nicely grouped together might make an ideal target for a fortnight's solo exploration.

My survival kit included pages from the railway timetable, a 1:500,000 Michelin road map, a guide to Portugal and a list of hotels. It was foolish of me not to include a dictionary and phrase book as virtually no one spoke English and I never came across a menu translated into English. This meant taking pot luck at restaurants. Portuguese is easier to read than to pronounce.

There are three Iberian broad gauge routes out of Oporto. The most important is the 211-mile Linha do Norte connecting Oporto with Libson. This line is electrified. There is one non-stop train per day, named the 'Cidade Invicta' in the up direction and the 'Sao Jorge' in the down direction. Both leave their starting points at 10.45 and take 3hr 12min for the jounrey and that is the best timing there is in Portugal. The Linha do Minho runs north for 93 miles to Monçao. There are two daily connections with Vigo via Valença. For motive power this line is served by English Electric Bo-Bo diesels or Budd dmus as far as Viana do Costelo. The best time for the 83miles from Oporto to Valença is 2hr 26min.

The Linha do Douro runs east to Barca de Alva,

Below: S. Bento station, Oporto, terminus for the Norte, Douro and Minho lines. On the right, a six-coach emu 'Regional' waits to depart for Coimbra and, on the left, a rake of stainless steel Budd coaches for the north, or a trip up the Douro Valley.

127 miles away on the Spanish frontier. After a preliminary skirmish through the countryside it settles down to hugging the granite banks of the River Douro, which due to the number of hydro-electric stations is more a series of reservoirs than anything recognisable as a river. The major tributaries on the north bank, the Tâmega, Corgo, Tua and Sabor all add to the stock of water. A metre gauge line follows each valley. There are therefore four sets of connections to be made and it is not surprising that the best journey time for the 127 miles of the Linha do Donro is just over five hours. Any tightening of the schedule might end in a knock-on disaster and throw the whole system out of gear. Trains on this route are diesel-hauled. Carriages are added at Campanhã on the outskirts of Oporto and removed at Régua by which point the number of passengers is somewhat diminished.

There are six totally unconnected metre gauge systems in north Portugal. The most important is the system which runs out of Oporto. After double-tracking for nearly 4 miles, the line splits. The shorter arm runs north to the seaside resort of Pávoa de Varzim, which is 15 miles further, then cuts across country for about 19 miles to meet the Minho line at Famalicão. The other branch heads first north, then east, and serves Guimarães and Fafe, 52 miles distant. I suspect that this system does more business than all

the other five combined and it has therefore received nearly all the new equipment. Smart red and white dmus of French origin, their angular appearance betraying their country of origin, provide an efficient service, helped out by older rolling stock hauled by Alsthom Bo-Bo diesel locomotives. Steam has disappeared.

Four lines, looking like a row of wind buffeted reeds on the map, rely on the Douro line. Each takes its name after the river to which it owes its allegiance. Nearest Oporto is the Tâmega line which climbs up from Livração to Amarante and after some 32½ miles at the village of Arco de Baulhe runs out of excuses for going any further. Next comes the Corgo line, climbing out of Regua to Vila Real and by the 97th kilometre (nearly 61 miles) has reached the spa town of Chaves on the Tâmega, and as this is in sight of the Spanish frontier there is no point in going further. The Tua line starts at Tua and after following the gorge for some distance runs through gentler country to serve Mirandela and finally Bragança, 84 miles distant. Last of the four is the Sabor line, starting at Pocinho (where they are squeezing in yet another hydro-electric station on the Douro), climbs away from the River Sabor as quickly as it can, manages to get to Moncorvo successfully, misses Mogaduro by about 4 miles and finally, after wandering across the altiplano, runs out

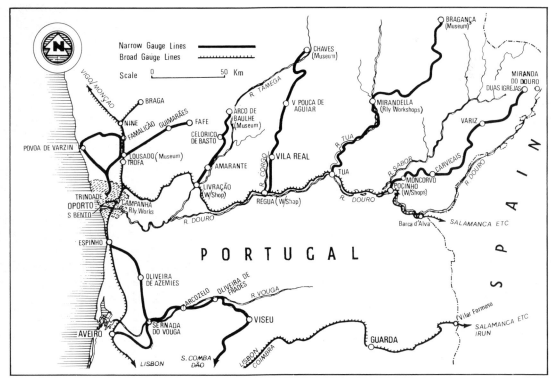

of track 7 miles before reaching Miranda do Douro, which is the only possible reason for having come this far. The village terminus, Duas Igrejas (two churches), is 66 miles from Pocinho. The last metre gauge system is to the south and serves Viseu. You can catch a railcar either from the seaside town of Espinho, in which case the distance is 88 miles, or from Aveiro further down the coast, in which case the distance is 71 miles. The two lines meet at Sernada do Vouga. From Viseu you can backtrack for 31 miles to Santa Comba do Dão from which there is a broad gauge connection to Coimbra. These six lines comprise the system which I set out to explore.

There is a difficulty in imposing a corporate image on rolling stock which is up to 67 years old and motive power up to 90 years old without making these older items look ridiculous. However, the CP logo which resembles the Canadian National motif is applied where possible.

Wednesday, 9 May 1979

British Airways Flight 402 lands on time at Pedras Rubras airport. The day is cloudless and hot, more summer than spring. I find that I am the only passenger on the airport bus and by the end of the journey conclude that seasoned travellers go by taxi. However, the 10p journey is quite acceptable. I select a pensão in the Avenida dos Aliados, also favoured by cafés and ironmongers. My sixth floor room overlooks the Avenida and that night I discover that a red and blue neon sign flashes just outside the window. My

first task is to visit the tourist office in the town hall at the top of the Avenida. They supply me with a plan of Oporto and kindly mark the locations of restaurants. Behind the town hall is a no man's land and here I find the Trinidade station which serves Pávoa and Fafe. It reminds me of an open-air municipal swimming pool filled with granite chips. Why are there no platform canopies? The dmus are modern. On a siding I see several carriages which are rather ancient. Are they abandoned or due for preservation? Walk back down the Avenida to the Praca da Liberdade. Oporto's last trams enter bottom right, circle the equestrian statue of Dom Pedro IV and then head out again for Foz on the coast. São Bento, the main terminus, is just off the square, the booking hall decorated with blue and white azulejos. Eight platforms cut off in their prime by a cliff can only accommodate six carriages each. The station is too short and points the wrong way. I walk down the Rua das Flores lined with charming but no longer fashionable shops to the bridges over the river which are to Oporto what the Eiffel Tower is to Paris. Eiffel designed the graceful Dona Maria rail bridge, which is nine years older than the high and low deck Dom Luis I road bridge at the foot of which I am standing. I climb the steps lined with houses which look incongruous under the steel structure of the approach spans.

Thursday, 10 May

I take the train to Barcelos in order to photograph the weekly market. The train runs through delightful countryside, which is not so much agricultural as market garden. Some fields are no bigger than a suburban plot. There is a lot of ploughing with oxen teams, rotavators are at work and when the field is too small for either, hoes are used. Each field is surrounded by vines cantilevered out from granite uprights. Pine and eucalyptus woods are everywhere. Barcelos market lives up to its reputation. Vegetables, chickens, shoes and clothing exist in profusion as well as local pottery and carved wood yokes, which would make very nice bedheads. I lunch on the terrace of a restaurant overlooking the River Cavedo. The bridge over it is narrow, two lorries meet in the middle and the traffic

Left: The box girder bridge over the Rive Ave carrying the Minho and Fafe lines. Mixed broad and metre gauge track is combined for nearly a mile. This is a broad gauge train, headed by one of the English Electric Bo-Bo diesel electrics.

Top right: An Allan railcar prepares to reverse into sidings at Sernada do Vouga. Here the track to Aveiro crosses a combined road and rail bridge over the River Vouga.

Right: 'The train about to leave for Viseu from the turntable . . .' at Sernada do Vouga, replacing a similar unit which had brought me from Aveiro. A 1940s' railbus with a temperamental Chevrolet engine.

builds up behind on each side. The situation is not sorted out until the end of the meal. I take a train on to Viana do Costelo. On the way back I spot a tank engine in a shed at Nine, the junction for Braga. It is connected by some sort of umbilical cord to the building, maybe a water pipe. This is the only broad gauge steam engine I am to see. Presumably it is in working order.

Friday, 11 May

Catch one of the angular metre gauge dmus to Guimarães. Each station along the way appears to have one ancient carriage as a nostalgic reminder of things past. Most are on their last legs. However, if all were assembled and refurbished it would make a very appealing train for Sunday enthusiasts. Guimarães, the cradle of Portugal, as it is called, offers some very good subjects for photography. In fact, looking back, it gets my award for the town with the best historic character. On to Fafe. The train climbs to a summit of 388m (1,261ft) before dropping again to a pleasant town, in which I am able to spend only an hour. On the way back I see a row of metre gauge steam engines at Lousada, a station shared by both gauges. I make a quick decision and leave the train and inspect them. They are very rusty and one of them is a powerful Henschel 2-8-2T. There is also a building marked 'Seccao Museologica' which is locked.

The metre gauge rails are laid on the same sleepers as the broad gauge between Lousada and Trofa. An intriguing situation. There is a path beside the rails

which I follow to the box girder bridge over the River Ave and then climb to the road before reaching Trofa.

Saturday, 12 May

Book to Braga but break the journey at Famalicão for a quick there-and-back to Pávoa de Varzim. The rails continue from Famalicão down to Lousada but no passenger services are run. The track also sits between the broad gauge rails. Perhaps it is used occasionally for goods traffic. Ticket inspection in Portugal is carried out on trains and the inspector makes his rounds between every station. On this occasion it was made clear to me that a break of journey is not allowed. Braga has trolleybuses and the best municipal gardens I have ever seen.

Sunday, 13 May

By emu from Sao Bento to Espinho. The train reverses at Campanhã and crosses the single-track Maria Pia bridge at a walking pace. The track is 172ft above the river. The sand dunes along the coast are lined with cars. I find Espinho shabby and depressing. The Allan railcar from Espinho to Sernada takes two hours to cover the 39 miles, a pleasant journey mainly through eucalyptus woods. The *cantina* at the station is full of TV addicts watching one of the Grand Prix races. I ask the stationmaster, who fortunately speaks some French, whether I may walk over to two tank engines and I am invited to inspect the workshops as well. One of the engines is being used as a kettle in order to hose

Above: Two of the three Borsig 4-6-0Ts dumped behind the CP bus workshops at Viseu, awaiting scrapping; Nos E124 leading and E133 behind.

Below: This venerable coach seen at Chaves is probably the oldest passenger-carrying vehicle still in service on the North Portuguese metre gauge; its builder's plate reads Caminhos de Ferro do Minho e Douro, Officinas Geraes, Campanha, 1912.

Right: Only the Mallets survive as train hauling steam locomotives on the Portuguese metre gauge. This 0-4-4-0T taking water at Amarante was heading a Sunday evening return excursion on the Tamega line.

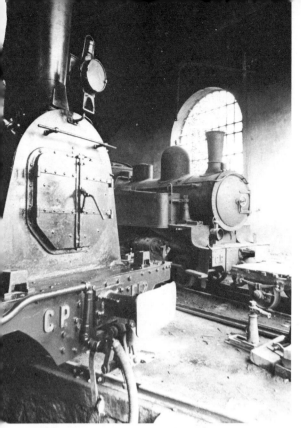

Left: Pocinho station, on the Sabor line, on a Sunday morning. Broad gauge train on the left for Oporto. The mixed train on the right headed by a Henschel 2-4-6-0T Mallet, No E206, built 1913, is awaiting to depart for Duas Igrejas.

Above: The only railway museum without doors is at Bragança, on the Tua line. Esslingen 0-6-0T No E52 of 1889 is on the left, with Decauville 2-6-0T No E95 on the right.

Above right: Bragança station with an Alsthom diesel ready to take a mixed train down to Tua.

Below: Pocinho station and another view of E206 on the mixed train to Duas Igrejas, also seen (left).

down a railcar. Portuguese Railways (CP) also provide bus services and I catch a Rodovia bus down to Aveiro. Each station has a newly-built bus shelter looking like an agricultural building. Back to Oporto by *rapido*.

Monday, 14 May

This is the real beginning of my survey of metre gauge lines and I start with the southernmost, that to Viseu. From Aveiro I take one of the more ancient railbuses built at Sernada some thirty years ago. Looking very much like a bus it has a Chevrolet engine. The bodywork is the worse for wear and is painted several shades of blue. At one point the starter refuses to work. The stronger passengers get out and give it a push. At Sernada everyone has to change to an identical bus. Out of the corner of my eye I see one of the tank engines setting out with flat trucks loaded with ballast. Soon, the second bus is in trouble. It appears to be overheating. The radiator is topped up at every station from a watering can. At one point the

engine is hosed down, without ill effect. We reach the summit at 533m (1,733ft) and after that descend easily to Viseu.

Tuesday, 15 May

I make a brief excursion down the Dão branch in the hope of finding a suitable location for photographing wild flowers. Jump off at a halt called Porto da Lage, an idyllic spot with a stream running through pinewoods, and this gives just enough time to take photographs before catching the same railcar back to Viseu.

Wednesday, 16 May

From Viseu to Regua by bus, a 57-mile journey over moorland. The metre gauge train to Vila Real is headed by an Alsthom diesel coupled to a number of bogie goods wagons followed by three MAN carriages dating from the 1920s. There is time to inspect a Henschel 0-4-0T built in 1922, which was rescued from the

scrapheap and is now used for shunting. The driver obligingly runs it backwards and forwards so that I may photograph it in motion. The train does the 16 miles in fifty minutes, gaining nearly 1,300ft in height.

The Mateus palace (as pictured on the bottle) is 2 miles outside the town of Vila Real. I take a taxi there and I am told by a stern lady that I must go on a guided tour of the inside before wandering round the beautifully-kept formal gardens. The stables are being used as a kindergarten and the chapel can be booked for weddings. I walk back to the Mateus factory in the hope of buying some wine but this proves impossible.

Thursday, 17 May

I arrive at the station to find there is a national 24-hour

Above: Moncorvo, Sabor line, with the unique Giesl-fitted Henschel 2-4-6-0T Mallet No E209 heading a down mixed train.

Below: A Sunday evening excursion at Amarante, bound for Livraçao, headed by Henschel 0-4-4-0T Mallet No E161.

rail strike in progress. This is a very orderly strike. Workers' demands have been printed and pinned up on the station building. The station master is not on strike and allows me to put my bags in his office. This gives me time to walk round the botanical gardens where young delinquents are carrying out therapeutic hedge-clipping under the direction of a guard. The strike finishes at midday and I catch the train to Chaves. The summit is at Vila Pouca and, at 2,372ft, is the highest point reached on any of the six metre gauge systems. At Chaves there is another museum. The station master unlocks the doors to reveal an Esslingen 0-6-0T, built in 1889, a Hohenzollern 0-6-0T, built in 1904 and a Henschel 0-6-6-0T, built in 1911, but there is no information as to their working life or how they came to be here, not even in Portuguese. All three are in perfect condition.

In the shed is a Henschel Mallet 2-4-6-0T built in 1923, which no doubt could be pressed into service should one of the diesels fail. A first-class carriage in the station bears the plate 'Caminhos de Ferro do Minho e Douro 1912'.

Friday, 18 May

Rather than retrace my steps to Regua, I take a bus to Bragança. Here, in a semi-circular shed at right-angles to the station platform are three more locomotives: an Esslingen 0-6-0T, which has lost its maker's plate to souvenir hunters, so a conversation in German reveals; a Henschel 0-4-4-0T, built in 1908 and a Decauville 2-6-0T, built in 1910. The shed might become a museum if only they can fit some doors. In the evening I am invited into the hotel kitchen to sit with the family and watch television.

Below: A Geraes railbus of 1948 and a Nohab railcar meet at Amarante station. These two types do the bulk of the passenger work on the Tamega line.

Saturday, 19 May

This is my longest day's journey. It takes me nearly twelve hours to cover the 170 miles down to Tua, along the broad gauge Douro line to Pocinho, and then on the Sabor metre gauge up to Duas Igrejas and it costs £2.40. The train down to Tua is diesel-hauled, but there is a glimpse of steam at Mirandela, where the workshops are situated.

There is plenty of time to wander round the yard at Pocinho. Plenty of steam here, including an Esslingen 0-6-0T of 1889 and four more Henschel 0-4-4-0Ts. However, the last leg of the journey is completed in a 25-seater Gerais-built railbus of 1948 which looks like a blue woodlouse. Protocol is rigidly observed throughout the journey, the driver not putting the engine in gear until given the go-ahead by the conductor. Over the driving position is a notice which reads 'He who talks to the driver must hold himself responsible for causing a disaster through distraction'. No one takes any notice. For the last half-hour I am the only passenger and begin to have visions of a cold and uncomfortable night at Duas Igrejas. However, there is an old Mercedes taxi driven by one Eduardo who takes me to a hotel in Miranda. The hotel is practically filled up by a coach-load of tourists and this is the only time I have any anxiety about finding a room.

Sunday, 20 May

My target is Amarante on the Tamega line, the final link in the chain. Livração, the starting point for this line, has two Henschel 0-4-4-0Ts at its disposal but we make the journey in a Nohab-built railcar. Enquiries at Amarante station about the *vapor* reveals that a steam train is due down at about 20.00. Just as it is getting too dark to take any photos it appears, a Henschel with one green and two red carriages. This must be an excursion train.

Monday, 21 May

My ambition to ride a steam train is fulfilled in an unexpected way. I am given permission to ride in the first-class carriage attached to the morning goods train headed for Arco de Baulhe. After scraping at the maker's plate of the carriage it turns out to be a Van Der Zypen and Charlier of 1925 vintage. It rains to begin with and the journey is very leisurely including a long break for lunch. By the time we get to Arco the weather has cleared, but the station master insists on taking his umbrella when showing me his treasures, a 1905 Henschel and two four-wheeled Royal coaches, built in Germany and France in the first decade of the century. The ballast here includes white quartz and I pocket a sample.

Tuesday, 22 May

My day off. Spend most of it in the tea-shops which line the banks of the Tamega and which sell sticky, sweet cakes. The river here is treated as a real amenity, in sharp contrast to Chaves, upstream, which uses it as a garbage dump.

Wednesday, 23 May

This is my last day and I have to get back to Oporto. I allow myself the luxury of a first-class ticket, which entitles me to sit beside the driver in the Gerais railbus. The short wheelbase makes going round curves a painful affair.

What is the future of the metre gauge lines? Will lack of equipment, lack of passengers, or better road services oblige CP to close the less profitable lines? Steam services are still operating on two lines and steam is available on three others. There is an instinct for preservation as the little museums show. What chance is there for more imaginative use of the Portuguese narrow gauge?

Below: Henschel 0-4-4-0T No E161 taking water at a station beyond Amarante, at the head of a train which was mixed as far as Amarante and freight only to Arco de Baúlhe. A 1925 Van der Zypen & Charlier clerestory first-class coach is next the engine.

From Crewe to Jerusalem

PAUL COTTERELL

It is not so very often that one sees articles dealing with the rolling stock of a particular railway, and when the railway concerned happens to be overseas, and defunct into the bargain, then the chances of seeing any such thing in print is extremely rare. It's not every day, though, that one has the opportunity to report on the continued existence of pre-nationalisation and *pre-Grouping* passenger and goods vehicles in Britain, let alone in such an unlikely country as Israel! But first, a bit of history.

Before independence Israel was part of the mandated territory of Palestine, and before this it was an almost totally neglected province of the Turkish Ottoman Empire. During World War 1 the British Army conquered Palestine, ending almost exactly four centuries of misrule by 'the Unspeakable Turk'. In so doing, the British built the major part of a modest network of lines which was to serve the country throughout the uneasy thirty years or so of Britain's mandate, and which was then inherited — through blood and fire — by Israel Railways.

Having laid the tracks the British needed something to run upon them. What more natural than to import the necessary equipment from home? A most interesting and antiquated selection of steam engines was shipped out (of which, more anon), and thirty bogie passenger coaches were despatched around the same time, along with numerous goods wagons; this was in 1916 or thereabouts. Of the carriages, seventeen came from the Midland Railway and another thirteen had been requisitioned from the London and South Western Railway. These numbers, incidentally, may be queried. Certain British sources state that the figures were sixteen and twelve respectively, but I have made use of Palestine Railways' records which are consistent in giving the first quantities mentioned.

These coaches arrived in Palestine as ambulance vehicles, their former histories seemingly lost or buried somewhere among the files in England, for PR appear never to have made reference to details of their previous identities beyond a vaguely worded phrase to the effect that they had been built sometime just after the turn of the century. The Midland examples were non-clerestoried and appear to have been suburban stock of David Bain's design. If anyone reading this can furnish particulars of their original identities then I would be most interested.

Once the war was over there was no longer any reason for the coaches to remain as ambulances and they were converted for ordinary use, thereby becoming the first passenger stock to be owned by the newly-formed Palestine Railways. (Some Egyptian coaches had been on hire to tide the Railways over in the meantime.) The Midland carriages, while not up to the magnificence of that company's main line stock, were certainly superior to the LSWR specimens, and several were rebuilt to first-class, while others became composites or all-thirds. The South Western examples did not aspire to a more exalted position than third-class.

The years passed and times changed. Other coaches arrived from English builders to share in the working of the daily rumble from Haifa to Kantara on the Suez Canal (a train which, for decades, boasted Wagons-Lits diners and sleepers), or from Jaffa along the rather spectacular line — originally metre gauge, then 3ft 5ins (1,050mm), then partly 2ft gauge (600mm), before finally being standard gauged! — through the Judean mountains to Jerusalem. Passengers of all sorts endured dusty and soporific journeys: British Colonial officers in first-class compartments on soft leather seats; Arab businessmen travelling from Damascus to Cairo in the seconds; Jewish immigrants and Bedouin (the latter sometimes with a whole menagerie of livestock ranging from chickens to baby camels) on hard wooden slats in the third-class. Many of the Midland coaches were further transformed down the years. Two became saloons for the convenience of railway officers and their guests, and a couple of others were fitted out with buffets for varying lengths of time. The South Western lot steered a more humdrum course and saw much less in the way of renovations.

Things might have gone on in this fairly timeless sort of way but for the growing spectre of political unrest. In 1936 the 'Disturbances' broke out and some of our carriages were badly bashed about by Arab terrorists in what was really an insurrection. A few of the Midland and LSW coaches were so extensively damaged that they were written-off. In 1939 world war came again (during which Palestine Railways were burdened with an enormous influx of traffic and vehicles), and after that, more war.

In 1948 the modern Jewish state of Israel was established and the 'Old Contemptibles' of this story came under foreign command. Israel being an egalitarian society, all the coaches taken over from the British administration were immediately reduced to the ranks — classless travel being a feature of Israel Railways occasionally remarked upon by tourists and other newcomers who bother to go by train and have

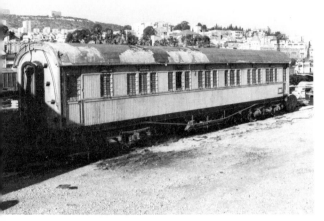

Left: An ex-Midland Railway coach at Haifa in the spring of 1978. *Author*

Below left: The Palestine Railways' erstwhile pay coach, of LSWR origin, at Haifa diesel depot in March 1977. *Author*

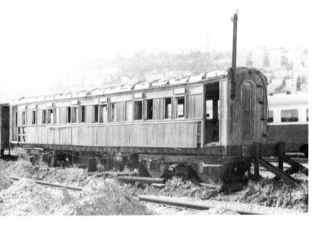

saw it not so long ago. This is PR No 77, which had been rebuilt by Palestine Railways into a pay coach. In this form it once featured in a Wild-West type of escapade when it was attacked and robbed by Jewish 'bandits', in 1946! The second is No 316 which now lanquishes on a short length of track in Haifa port. The fourth member of this venerable quartet is the erstwhile first-class No 103, another of the Midland carriages. It is in use as a stores coach at the former narrow gauge Hedjaz Railway engine shed in Haifa, and is in the best condition of the four. Both No 103 and the anonymous one at Lod still carry their Midland Railway works plates. It is a pity that Derby did not see fit to stamp them with the date of construction.

While the passenger coaches must claim most of the attention, mention of goods vehicles is not out of place. As is only to be expected these are by no means so well documented, but enough remains, either in print or actually on rails, to show that a vast selection of strange and exotic wagons has trundled over the metals of Palestine and Israel Railways, the greatest proportion arriving in World War 2. Echoed in the files or on builders' plates are such far away places as Java, Italy, Hong Kong and the USA. Locally, Syrian, Iraqi and Turkish freight stock was well represented, as also, of course, was that of Egypt. Of more homely sound to British ears were the names of companies like the Great Central, LNER, Great Western and Southern. The stuff that arrived from England was usually of a more inferior sort, generally conforming to the lamentable contemporary British standards of loose-coupled, unfitted rattle-traps. Various examples of these are dotted about the herbiage of Qishon works, in several stages of decrepitude; Colonel Stephens would have loved this place!

But getting back to those splendid old passenger carriages. There is vague talk of establishing a proper railway museum in Israel. I have done my best to prod the issue regularly at headquarters but, so far, with no concrete results. Israel Railways are living on a shoestring budget and heaven knows where the necessary money would come from to set up a museum. In the meantime, I am reliably informed that the Midland and LSWR coaches are being held in reserve for possible preservation. The trouble is that they are all out in the open and won't last for ever without a modicum of care, be it just a roof over their heads. British enthusiasts have been importing a lot of continental steam engines and other equipment just lately. Wouldn't it be nice to have a whip-round and

been used to a choice in the standard of comfort and privacy they are prepared to pay for. Slowly but surely, modern German, French and Jugoslav-built carriages arrived to oust the wooden-bodied ex-PR coaches from passenger service. But there was still plenty of life left in their ageing, somewhat calcined, bones. The bodies of several were lifted off their bogies and now serve as offices at Qishon workshops. One of the Midland saloons thus treated still sports its early Palestine Railways interior fittings — even H. G. Wells could not have conjured up a more entertaining mode of time-travel! Others were gutted inside but remained on their wheels and served out their time as departmental vehicles. Wonderful to relate, four of these ancient British coaches now well over seventy years of age, are still knocking about, though rather unsteady on their legs and rarely moved.

An unidentifiable Midland survivor is out to grass on a siding at Lod, cheek by jowl with an Egyptian State Railways coach, one of several which the Israelis captured in the Sinai Campaign of 1956. At Haifa are two mobile examples of the LSW exiles (still with their wooden centred Mansell wheels), one of which was parked at the back of the diesel depot the last time I

do the same for one or two of the coaches? After all, their pedigrees are immaculate, real English thoroughbreds, and they would make a fine sight at, say, Butterley or on the Watercress Line. Otherwise I'm afraid, like the old soldiers that they are, they are likely to fade away.

Earlier, I made a passing reference to former British steam engines in Palestine. I shall confine mention almost entirely to engines sent out from British railways, excluding those which were built in Britain especially for Palestine. Nor is it possible to give more than the merest hint of the magnificently miscellaneous, and sometimes exotic, collection of engines which once worked there.

Considering its tiny size Israel has had a fascinating network of very varied railway lines at one time or another. Not that one would imagine so now, judging from the present miniscule system. World War 1 saw the peak of railway building activity, in what was then Palestine. At first it was the Turks who constructed a series of lines in support of their inept efforts to capture or incapacitate the Suez Canal. These adventures goaded the British into wresting Palestine from the feeble grip of Turkey. Early in 1916 the British began their advance from Egypt, laying down a standard gauge railway from Kantara on the Canal which was to keep abreast of the British Army for the next two and a half years until Haifa was reached and the Turks finally booted out of the country. The line from Kantara, by the way, has not been open in its entirety for over thirty years, except for one Israeli expeditionary train which crept past the pot-holes and mines of the Sinai section just after the Six Day War of 1967. The long-awaited, and recently concluded peace settlement with Egypt may well see tracks relaid and the line back in action.

The first engines to work on this military line were mobilised from Egyptian stock. This was no more than an emergency stop-gap and the British soon cast about for a more lasting solution to the motive power problem. But a locomotive in wartime was then almost worth its weight in gold, and the best that could be conjured up was hardly what the troops would have chosen. New engines were out of the question so some old-timers, prised from the jealous hands of English railways, would have to suffice. From the London and South Western came thirty-six of William Adams' '0395' 0-6-0s, built between 1881-85 by Neilson's of Glasgow. The first half-dozen were shipped in September 1916 and the last lot departed the shores of Blightly in April 1918. Later in the same year ten were transferred to Mesopotamia (now Iraq), of which three returned to Palestine in 1919, the other seven being taken into Iraqi State Railways stock. In 1920 Palestine Railways were formed and the twenty-nine Adams 0-6-0s in Palestine at this time became PR

property. Most had been sold for scrap by 1928 but seven were to remain in shunting service until about 1936 when they were replaced by some new Nasmyth Wilson 0-6-0Ts. Even this was not quite the end of the road for they were then used as buffer-stops in various sidings until finally succumbing to the breaker's hammer at the end of World War 2. In their last years these South Western engines must have provided a delightfully rustic and unexpected bonus for any passing enthusiast.

Although the LSWR 0-6-0s were hardly in the first bloom of youth when they went to war, they were less pensionable than some of their contemporaries which came to help in the conquest of the Holy Land. These were forty-two Webb 'Coal Engines' from the London and North Western Railway, the first of which emerged from Crewe in 1873. Five hundred of these 0-6-0s were built up to 1892 so, presumably, the loss of forty-two was not such a blow to the LNWR as was felt by Eastleigh when half the '0395s' were mobilised.

Were the righteous Francis Webb still around at the time he would doubtless have been mortified to learn that his products were to prove less durable than those of Adams, in Palestine at least, for the LNWR locomotives did not survive beyond 1922. The South Western 0-6-0s always seem to have been preferred for the more onerous duties, the 'Coal Engines' generally

Two types of locomotives sent out to Palestine in World War I. *Below:* LSWR Adams '0395' No 398. *Ian Allan Library. Bottom:* LNWR 'Coal Engine' 0-6-0 No 2200. *LPC*

Above: Great Central 'ROD' 2-8-0 WD No 9726 (later No 70726) came off the road on the Haifa-Beirut line. *K. R. M. Cameron*

pottering about on odds and ends. A fairly typical sort of duty for the North Western locomotives was the working of a disinfector train. (Bugs, of several obnoxious varieties, are endemic in the Sinai Desert — many Israeli soldiers came back from the Yom Kippur War still scratching.) In October 1920 ex-LNWR No 3320, with Driver Mustafa and Fireman Khaled, was in charge of fumigation, covering little more than 600 miles during the month. Not that the South Western 0-6-0s were beneath this turn of duty, but as a rule their existence was sweeter.

Among various miscellaneous standard gauge engines taken over by the Palestine Military Railways in World War 1 were six Manning Wardle 0-6-0Ts. Four of these (later PR Nos 26-29) had been built in 1917 for the Inland Waterways and Docks Dept, and eventually became Israel Railways locomotives in 1948. The other pair (Nos 30 and 99) dated from 1902 and 1900 respectively. They had previously belonged to the contractors, J. Aird & Co. Neither was to survive the sun and heat for very long: No 30 went in 1928, while No 99 appears to have expired without even being taken over by Palestine Railways.

Apart from the Kantara-Haifa standard gauge line, which the British laid to supply their ponderous advance into Palestine, several narrow gauge railways were also constructed. Some of the 60cm gauge lines saw American-built engines in the shape of Baldwin 4-6-0Ts, while a few Hunslet 4-6-0Ts were supplied for the 2ft 6in gauge. It would seem that the latter arrived too late to see active military service, but a trio of Hunslets was afterwards in the employ of the Palestine Electric Corporation, being lettered with the Hebrew initials of that company.

Between the wars Palestine Railways settled down as well as circumstances were to allow. New engines arrived from Britain every once in a while to share the meagre services with the Baldwin 4-6-0s that were built in 1918 and soon swept the South Western and

LNW 0-6-0s from the scene. It was not until World War 2 however, that genuinely British locomotives were again to put in an appearance in Palestine. An overwhelming increase of traffic made their introduction a vital necessity. First of the War Department engines to arrive, in March 1942, were some of John Robinson's celebrated Great Central 2-8-0s. They really came into their own in 1944 when they took over much of the traffic on the Haifa-Beirut-Tripoli line, most of which had been constructed in 1942, giving Palestine its only (and very fleeting) standard gauge outlet to the north. The 'RODs' were well-liked locally, being considered real workhorses, but they had their drawbacks. The regulators were very stiff and insensitive and more than one over-eager driver started away without his train, to the accompaniment of a musical 'ping' from the snapped coupling or tender pin.

One rather interesting, if incidental, feature of the Robinson 2-8-0s was their livery. Before shipping to the Middle East the War Department had them outshopped in grey. Against a background of glaring sand they presented a peculiarly spectral appearance. A gradual reversion to black was made as they went through shops at such places as Qishon (Haifa), Jaffa and Suez.

None of these 2-8-0s was permanently taken over by PR, though one (WD No 70745) was dumped at Haifa and could still be seen there as late as 1952. More than thirty are known to have worked in Palestine at some time or other, though there were constant comings-and-goings of all the WD locomotives and the situation was fluid. Transfers were frequent, in particular to and from Egypt, making compilation of comprehensive lists a hazardous undertaking.

Considerably more modern than the 'RODs' were the Stanier '8F' 2-8-0s, of which at least fifty-three were in Palestine at varying periods during the 1939-45 war. If the drawing up of a list for the GC 2-8-0s is fraught with obstacles, then it is doubly difficult to trace the whereabouts of the '8Fs'. Many seem to have been peripatetic and loathe to stay in one place, while others were simply stored in Palestine towards the end of the war before being shipped home. However, twenty-four were permanent residents, being officially on hire to Palestine Railways, and all except one of these became Israel Railways' engines in 1948. The exception certainly did lead a forlornly sedentary existence, but her citizenship was much in dispute. This was WD No 70372 which was isolated at Tulkarm when Jordan invaded the West Bank during Israel's war of independence. And there she remained for more than twenty years, rusting slowly, a haven for wildlife and snipers. The cavalry finally arrived in 1967 when Israel conquered the West Bank, but for

No 70372 there was to be no happy ending. Israel had been steamless since 1959 and as the '8F' was too far-gone for serious thought of preservation she was released from her prolonged purgatory a few years after liberation.

One or two other '8Fs' were to gain renown under the auspices of Israel Railways. A sparkling WD No 70513 hauled IR's inaugural regular passenger train, between Haifa and Hadera, in January 1949; before this date the Israelis had been able to run no more than the very occasional passenger turn because of sporadic fighting. In 1958, No 70414 became the subject of a popular Israeli song after heading the last steam train from Beersheba on the recently completed line to the 'capital' of the Negev Dersert.

Not surprisingly, the LMS 2-8-0s had a wholesome reputation in Israel, though they were never called upon to perform the same feats of haulage as they were wont to do in the desperate days of World War 2. For several months during that conflict '8Fs' had thundered up to Artuf (now Bet Shemesh) with 800 tons of freight for Jerusalem. This line was originally metre gauge and when the British relaid it to standard gauge in 1918 they omitted to straighten out the ferocious curves. Eight-coupled engines were not welcomed on the mountain section from Artuf, so here the '8F' would thankfully relinquish her load, leaving a trio of Baldwin 4-6-2Ts to sort out the final sinuous $22\frac{1}{2}$ mile-long slog, nearly all at 1 in 50, through the desolate Judean mountains to Jerusalem.

Eight-coupled locos were never entirely comfortable on the rails of PR. As usual the pw department blamed the locomotive people for a spate of nasty kinks in the track. Naturally enough, the motive power operators indignantly replied that the permanent way department should put its own house in order. One wonders, then, just who was responsible for giving a trial to a 2-10-0! Five of the large Riddles Austerity engines found their way to wartime Syria and one of them was once sent down to Lydda (Lod) with a night freight. My informant, Max Seidenberg, was responsible for turning it on the Lydda triangle, and a mighty protracted business it was. The 2-10-0 evidently made it back to Syria without causing too much trouble along the way. And there it stayed.

Palestine Railways were hard put to keep their locomotives running, even in what passed as peacetime in that country. During the war it was necessary to convert practically all the engines then on PR to oil-burners and this included the War Department 'ROD' and '8F' 2-8-0s. The system chosen was not of the best and required much supplementary work to give anything approaching satisfaction. But this was nothing compared to the chaos caused by abominable water. Scores of sorely needed engines were laid up with 'upset tummies', having ignored the injunction not to drink the local water. Even the best engines, among which the British ones could certainly be counted, were no match for this debilitating affliction. Bad water was to contribute to the early demise of steam on IR. Perhaps it may be some small comfort to lovers of British steam locomotives to know that the '8Fs' were among the last to turn a wheel in Israel.

When referring earlier to the old British rolling stock still to be found in Israel I bemoaned the lack of a railway museum in the country. While nothing of a practical nature has been done at least people are still talking about such a project. One idea, which certainly appeals to this writer, is for the import of a Turkish '8F', or possibly one of the American-built 'Middle East' 2-8-2s which actually worked in wartime Palestine and remain in service in Turkey. Thought has been given to running an occasional steam train, in particular for tourists, on the Jerusalem line, which is definitely in need of such an infusion, having lately had its service cut to a miserable two trains a day, one to and from Tel Aviv, the other between Haifa and the Holy City. Picture an '8F' shouting her way up towards the venerable, biblical hills of Judea with, perhaps, a couple of wooden-bodied Midland and LSWR coaches immediately behind the tender. And, just to add contrast, the train might include one or two ex-BR Mk IIC vehicles with which Israel Railways startled their customers early in 1977. A mere pipe-dream? Undoubtedly — unless something is done pretty soon.

Below: A Stanier '8F' 2-8-0 in WD service at Jaffa, Palestine Railways. No 70308 has been modified by British Army engineers. It was taken into Israel Railways stock in 1948. *K. R. M. Cameron*

Preserved coaches on BR metals

CHANNEL ISLANDS BOAT EXPRESS

The sight of preserved locomotives at work on BR lines became a feature of the 1970s. Sometimes they were accompanied by privately-owned preserved coaches to enhance the spectacle of historic locomotives and liveries. These pages illustrate some of the variety presented by rolling stock of a bygone era.

Above: There was a memorable 'double' at Paddington station on the evening of 15 September 1979. In Platform 1 was the Travellers Fare 'Centenary Express' composed of vehicles from the National Railway Museum, York, and on Platform 2, the Great Western Society's Vintage Train of GWR coaches, returning from an excursion. In the background is an Inter-City 125 train. *Great Western Society*

Left: H. P. Bulmer Ltd's Pullman cars add to the effect made by *King George V* near Claydon, north of Banbury, on 2 October 1971. *R. J. Farrell*

Top right: King George V again, this time heading the Severn Valley Railway's train of GWR coaches on a charter train bound for Chester from Hereford on 23 April 1977. *David Eatwell*

Right: It was over thirty years previous since chocolate and cream GWR coaches formed Channel Islands boat trains from Paddington. Here the clock is put back on 8 July 1979 as the GW Society's Vintage Train traverses the Weymouth Tramway to the Quay. *Great Western Society*

Above: The Scottish Railway Preservation Society has used its historic coaches for excursions in England and Scotland. The train is seen here on the Bo'ness branch at Kinneil Colliery on 27 August 1978. *R. E. Ruffell*

Below: Coaches owned by Mr W. McAlpine and Flying Scotsman Enterprises, of BR, GWR, LMS, LNER and Great Eastern origin form *Flying Scotsman's* train en route from Carnforth to Dinting near Darwen, on 28 September 1979. *L. A. Nixon*

The Gresley 2-6-2 tanks

A. G. DUNBAR

It must be admitted by most railway enthusiasts that H. N. Gresley was the last of the really great locomotive engineers, and also the last of a long line of giants in this particular profession. Much has been written about his many types of engine, especially the Pacifics, but little has appeared in print regarding the 'V1' and 'V3' 2-6-2Ts. This was very likely because these machines were not used in any spectacular fashion, and since their forte was usually local working they were never in the public eye to the same extent as Gresley's more famous classes.

From Grouping the tank engines in service on the LNER or being built were of classes already in existence before 1923 and it was not until 1930 that the 'V1' 2-6-2Ts appeared, and in common with many other engines designed by Gresley were examples of his 'big engine' policy, being the heaviest of the type constructed in this country.

When first built, eyebrows were raised at the idea of three-cylinder propulsion being part and parcel of a tank engine design for local services and experts pointed out that the largest user of the type, the GWR, managed very well with only two cylinders. So the argument developed once again — was Gresley right in his ideas that three cylinders were the answer to all problems of locomotion?

Above: A smartly turned-out 'V1' 2-6-2T, No 2907. *LPC*

My own experience of the class was entirely in Scotland where the first of them were sent when new, and where, until 1935, the only examples could be found. That they were a godsend to the Scottish Area of the LNER is an understatement — the tank engines of ex-NBR design were rapidly reaching the sere and yellow stage. In any case, new rolling stock coming into use for local trains was heavier and longer trains were also required, both factors taxing the limited capabilities of the existing classes of engine. The 'V1s' were welcomed by the operating department, but the same could not be said for the locomotive men, who as usual viewed the newcomers with some suspicion, if not hostility.

This hostility, if it can be called such, was mainly due to the fact that for many years the North British enginemen had been accustomed to engines of moderate power and while these were suitable for the work they were called on to perform when new, they did not measure up successfully to the changed conditions in railway operating in the mid/late 1930s.

On introduction, the class was confined to suburban working in Scotland, principally around Glasgow and

113

Edinburgh, but later they were in use in the North Eastern Area and Great Eastern sections of the LNER.

On occasion, the view of Scottish observers has been that the work required of the 'V1s' north of the Border was never very onerous and did not compare with what they did on the Newcastle-Middlesbrough semi-fast services. While this may be so — and I would not try to denigrate the work performed in the north-east — it might be as well to consider what could constitute 'hard' work. In the Glasgow area the engines were called on to work up to 10 bogie coaches and while the mileage of individual journeys might not exceed 30, in some instances, especially at peak periods, the timings were very tight. With short intervals between trains every minute counted in the maintenance of schedules. That the 2-6-2Ts put in some hard work cannot be denied since it was the nature of the train services that stops were frequent. Time was lost on starting away from stations if weather conditions made operations difficult.

It is worth looking at the driving technique employed for the 'V1s' in order to put the record straight as regards the quality of the work they did. Brought up in their traditional method of driving, the older school of North British drivers believed in what they generally called the 'wee valve' method of driving. This involved only opening the jockey (or 'wee') valve of the regulator and generally working to a fixed cut-off. This certainly got the engine moving the train but was responsible for excessive coal and water being used which variations in the cut-off used might have saved. It was difficult to persuade the older men that this type of driving was worse than useless with the 'V1s'; they swore by their 'wee valve' and many of them would not even reduce the cut-off below 25-30% as they would advance all kinds of fantastic theories why they should not. None of these would stand up to any detailed analysis. Among the younger men, however, the usual method of working was with the wide-open regulator and early cut-offs around 15-17% mark and far better results came from this approach. Despite this, the older men would not change their ways and this was reflected in the differing coal consumption and maintenance requirements of similar engines worked under different conditions.

The coal consumption of engines worked in accordance with the 'wee valve' method was usually about 30-60% greater than those worked more expansively but, despite this, the authorities took no action. The engines worked on the 'wee valve' also took more mechanical punishment than the others and this was reflected in higher maintenance costs. It is doubtful if this effect on running expenses was ever costed by the management but it would have supplied some very interesting comparative figures.

Over the years since Nigel Gresley first introduced his first multi-cylindered engines, controversy has raged over his derived valve gear. Indeed, it would be true to say that more has been written and spoken of this aspect of his locomotive designs than of any other single feature.

Just why this controversy should have arisen is rather a mystery — the gear itself was mechanically sound and it fulfilled the work asked of it in service. Over the years I have read scores of accounts to the effect that the lack of maintenance of the gear was responsible for its shortcomings; on many occasions this accusation was entirely unsupported by any concrete proof.

In most Gresley designs, and in the engines under discussion, the equal lever, as it was called, passed between the frames at the front of the cylinders, and immediately under the smokebox door. On the footplating above the lever there was a door that lifted to allow access to the lever and inside cylinder cover. When the smokebox was cleaned out, much of the accumulated ash and cinder fell on access door and running plate, and it was often easiest for the man on the job to lift the door and let the ashes fall straight down.

But smokebox cinders are like carborundum, and act like a grinding paste. When mixed with the grease and oil on the lever pins wear resulted that would not otherwise have occurred.

All the pins on the derived gear were fitted for grease lubrication, having what were called Enot nipples on the end of the pins, and they were bored to allow the grease to penetrate to the bearing surface. After some time it was found that the heaviest wear took place on the pin at the top of the combination lever of the valve gear, as well as on the pin at the end of the smaller inside equal lever usually termed the 'two to one', which actuated the centre piston valve. This pin was never oil-lubricated and the grease tended to attract the smoke ash which increased the normal amount of wear. In my experience, the curious point about the gear was that the cumulative wear on all the pins was transferred to this point on the centre valve and was responsible for the over-travel that took place. When a centre valve 'over-travelled' this could be readily observed since at the back of the steam chest there was what the locomen called a 'pop' — in reality, a small guide for the valve spindle which was often found with the end knocked off. This was a sure sign that the valve travel was excessive. Although the causes for this might have been avoided, it was hardly realistic that a strict watch could be maintained every time the smokebox was cleaned and on every man doing the job. Also, there could have been slip-ups in greasing the pins, which with the 'V1s' was set to be done weekly, or twice weekly as required. The real nigger in the wood-pile was the smokebox ash, and as it was present all the time, no ready solution to the problem of its disposal was ever attempted.

The management no doubt appreciated that the derived valve gear gave trouble and it was very apparent during the war years when the engines were far more intensively worked. The standards of workmanship in prewar years could not be achieved during the war and after the rot set in it was difficult to stop.

The centre large-end was another debatable aspect of Gresley's designs, but over the years I found that if it was correctly fitted and careful attention was paid to oiling, it would give no more trouble than any other type. In the earlier days, the connecting and coupling rods and the centre large-end were fitted with pin syphons, and these served their purpose without much trouble. Later, in BR days, these were replaced by the LMS-type 'restrictors' which were screwed into the oil pipe inside the cups, and never gave the same satisfaction as the pin syphons. Here again, perhaps, the drivers' prejudices entered into this matter as well, since many of the men continually complained about the restrictors. Another contributory factor, after nationalisation, was the change in the white-metalling of the bushes in those parts mentioned. Previously, all bushes were of the usual brass with white-metal insets. This was changed to white-metal lining completely covering the brass, the idea being when wear took place the bush was withdrawn, remetalled and returned and was then fit for further service. The idea was sound, and did aim at ultimate economy in brasses, since with the old type after a certain amount of wear the brass was scrapped and renewed. However, as with many other good ideas the white-metal lining was destroyed on occasions and the engine then ran for several days with the brass only; the subsequent wear removed the serrated portion that kept the white metal in place, and so the brass had to be renewed. On the 2-6-2Ts the source of most trouble with the coupling-rod bushes took place with the right-hand trailing bush which always wore excessively before any of the others. In addition, the first axlebox to knock due to wear in the hornblock bearing surface was, once again, the right-hand trailing. Why this should be so was one of those minor mysteries that remain unexplained although I have seen — and heard — quite a number of theories advanced for this occurrence.

A word must be said regarding the firing technique employed with the 'V1s'. In this, as in other things, there were several schools of thought: one lot regarded the ideal as filling the firebox well up and firing behind the door only, allowing the engine to rattle the coal forward. Some practised the 'thin fire' method, usually attended too often for good steaming, while others steered a middle course and worked between the two

Above: 'V1' 2-6-2T No 2920 is in charge of an Edinburgh Waverley-Stirling train on 21 August 1937, near Dalmeny Junction. *E. R. Wethersett/Ian Allan Library*

extremes by keeping a moderately thick fire and trying to keep the brick arch really hot, which was one of the secrets of making a 'V1' steam well. The fellow who had built up a thick fire of 'green' coal contrived to drop the temperature of the arch, and then wondered why his steam pressure went back, especially if he put on the injectors indiscriminately. On the train services I was familiar with, the injectors were usually put on when steam was shut-off for a stop, and allowed to fill the boiler until a re-start was made when they were shut off until the next stop. This was sufficient to keep the water level at about three-quarter glass, and had the merit of lowering boiler pressure very little which was an asset in working.

Taken all in all, the Gresley 2-6-2Ts performed well on the sort of services they were employed on in Scotland and, at times, did well on more exacting work. At Parkhead shed, Glasgow, where most of the class was allocated, one turn in the shed's links commenced at 05.15 and continued throughout the day with four sets of men until 02.15 the next morning when the locomotive returned to the shed, to leave again at 05.15. For more than two years, one engine which came new to Parkhead, engine No 498 (later No 67643), performed this rather heavy diagrammed working and never once gave any trouble. It was never off service except for the usual washing-out, and periodical examinations.

As regards periodical examinations, the LNER standard examinations of valves and pistons and renewal of brasses were carried out at 20,000-mile intervals, but after the BR standard was introduced this was increased to 30,000 miles. In my own opinion — and of most of the men who worked these engines — this was a retrograde step.

Sixteen years have passed since the last of the class was scrapped but the 'V1s' and 'V3s' may be remembered as one of the post-Grouping designs of locomotive that put in useful work of a very non-spectacular nature maybe, but none the less valuable for that.

Summer Saturdays on the Somerset and Dorset

GILES TATTON-BROWN

Between Bath and Bournemouth can be traced what was once the Somerset and Dorset Joint line. Today tall grass hides the ballast of the trackbed, bridges have been removed and stations torn apart. All that remains is the memory. Green Park station in Bath is now a car park (but might one day aspire to better things), a small stream flows from under the north portal of Devonshire Tunnel, and gutted stations and signalboxes remain as stark ruins of a railway.

The Somerset and Dorset line was always a great line of character. It ran from Bath through superb rural scenery for the majority of its 71 miles. Only the small coalfield around Radstock and Midsomer Norton was of less picturesque surroundings. These small mining communities, 10 miles from Bath, seemed very out of place in Somerset and did not blend into the countryside as well as the stone quarries of Moorewood and Ham Wood with their enormous stone crushing plants. After climbing from Radstock to Masbury Summit in the Mendips at 800ft, the line dropped down to Shepton Mallet and Evercreech, the junction for Glastonbury and Highbridge, a single line

Above: LMS '2P' 4-4-0 No 40564 and BR '5' 4-6-0 No 73047 head the northbound 'Pines Express' out of Shepton Mallet on 29 March 1961. *G. A. Richardson*

branch that used to be the main line until the completion of the Bath extension in July 1874. Continuing south the lines passed through the lush green meadows of Thomas Hardy's Vale of Blackmore, past Templecombe, a Crewe of Wessex, and down the Stour Valley towards Blandford Forum. Bournemouth was finally reached over the heath of Broadstone and then by way of the London & South Western Railway through the pinewoods of Branksome to the terminal station in the west of the town.

Much of the line was steeply graded with many miles at 1 in 50 including 2 miles which climbed out of Bath to Combe Down Tunnel — a most unpleasant single-bore tunnel over a mile long and without ventilation shafts — and seven miles from Radstock to Masbury at an average gradient of 1 in 66. In the southbound direction there was also a final steep bank to Parkstone at 1 in 60, especially difficult since a run could not be made at it because of the sharp curve at

116

Right: LMS '5' 4-6-0 No 44830 enters Templecombe with the southbound 'Pines Express' on 30 June 1950.

Below: S&DJR '4F' No 44559 is piloted by LMS '2P' 4-4-0 No 40568 on a Bournemouth-Bradford Saturdays only train near Wellow on 28 July 1951.   *Geoffrey J. Jefferson*

Poole. In the northbound direction the climb from Evercreech to Masbury was equally severe. with only a small level section at Shepton Mallet. Assisting locomotives were usually needed on all these banks and after World War 2 the LMS '3F' 0-6-0Ts were largely used.

Much of this line was single, including the first four miles out of Bath to Midford, and seventeen miles between Templecombe and Blandford. So, this country jointly-owned line traversing the beautiful rural counties of Somerset and Dorset, with single line sections and steep banks, was costly and difficult for the operator and yet fascinating for the observer.

Most of the passenger traffic took the form of short three or four-coach local trains that plied in leisurely fashion between Bath, Templecombe and Bournemouth. There was also the daily 'Pines Express', a through restaurant car train from Bournemouth to Manchester. This train, somehow almost too majestic for this quiet country line, was made up of ten or twelve coaches and headed by a large passenger engine and usually a pilot. However on summer Saturdays, as well as the one 'Pines' in each direction, there were as many as ten other holiday expresses in each direction from towns and cities in the Midlands and North to Poole and Bournemouth for the Hampshire and Dorset coasts. With this enormous amount of extra traffic on a relatively small line, facilities were taxed to the limit. The single-line bottleneck between Bath and Midford was particularly

difficult. Generally, northbound morning trains reached Bath just in time for the engines to be turned and quickly prepared to head back to Bournemouth with the southbound holiday expresses. Everything in the timetable was precisely timed and delays and breakdowns could lead to enormous problems. As well as the problems of occupation on the single line sections, the heavy expresses had to be piloted over the steeply graded sections. Usually Bath (Green Park) depot provided locomotives to pilot southbound trains as far as Evercreech Junction. Then they joined others from Templecombe depot in an impressive line on the middle road at the junction, and one by one worked the northbound trains over the Mendips to Bath. As well as the regular summer Saturday through trains, relief trains often ran in connection with northern town holiday weeks and especially at the peak period of the last two Saturdays in July and the first two in August. There were also the local trains to be fitted in. Virtually no freight services ran on these days.

Before World War 2 a certain number of summer trains ran, but afterwards, and especially as a result of petrol rationing, there was a vast increase in holiday rail traffic to coastal resorts all over Britain. Bournemouth was no exception and in 1948 there were seven trains each way from places such as Bradford, Leeds, Nottingham, Lincoln and Sheffield, as well as the 'Pines Express' from Manchester. The Bradford train ran overnight leaving at 20.30, reaching Bath at 02.55 and after crossing the Mendips at dawn terminated at Bournemouth at 06.00.

For 1949 there were more train services: two other overnight services ran from Sheffield and Derby, the Lincoln train was extended to Cleethorpes and there were new trains serving Birmingham, Derby and Liverpool. There were also express services to Bristol. Usually there were about 12-17 Saturdays in the summer timetable extending from early June to mid-September, but not all the trains ran on every Saturday so that regular diagramming was difficult. Relief trains also had to be fitted in, most often at the peak times when there were already about twelve regular trains. On 4 August 1951, for example, four northbound reliefs were booked to Birmingham, Coventry, Walsall and Rose Grove. On this day a pigeon special was scheduled from Bath to Templecombe, to add further congestion to the line.

During the early years of the 1950s there was a continual increase in these holiday services which reached a peak in 1954. Thereafter, the monopoly of the railways for such traffic was gradually broken, first by express coach services and, then, with the ever-increasing growth in private cars. In 1954 there were 15 southbound trains, including four overnight expresses, and 12 northbound trains, as shown in Table 1.

Table 1 — S&D summer Saturday workings 1954 (14 Saturdays)

SOUTHBOUND

19 June-18 September (14 days operated)

		Bath (arr)	Bournemouth W. (arr)
20.30	ex-Bradford (F. Sq)	03.15	06.00
09.05	ex-Bristol	09.53	12.55
06.52	ex-Cleethorpes	14.10	16.48
07.50	ex-Bradford (F. Sq)	14.50	17.35
10.25*	ex-Manchester (L. Rd)	15.40	18.08
10.30	ex-Liverpool (L. St)	16.36	19.25
/10.38	ex-Manchester (L. Rd)		

19 June-11 September (13 days operated)

08.20	ex-Bristol	09.05	11.48
09.13	ex-Birmingham (New St)	11.55	14.55
07.35	ex-Nottingham (Mid)	12.26	15.14

3 July-4 September (10 days operated)

07.40	ex-Birmingham (New St)	10.30	13.17

10 July-28 August (8 days operated)

22.00	ex-Sheffield (Mid)	02.35	04.56
22.39	ex-Manchester (L. Rd)	04.10	06.44
09.40	ex-Sheffield (Mid)	14.30	17.15

24 July-4 September (7 days operated)

23.00	ex-Derby (Mid)	02.45	05.18

3 July-7 August (6 days operated)

10.30	ex-Liverpool (L. St)	16.25	19.04

* The 'Pines Express'

NORTHBOUND

19 June-18 September (14 days operated)

		Bath (arr)
09.25	to Manchester (L. Rd), Liverpool (L. St)	11.41
09.45*	to Manchester (L. Rd)	11.56
09.55	to Leeds (City)	12.25
10.05	to Cleethorpes	12.45
11.12	to Derby (Mid)	13.49
11.40	to Sheffield (Mid)	14.10
19.25	to Bristol	21.53

19 June-11 September (13 days operated)

14.45	to Bristol	17.11

3 July-11 September (11 days operated)

08.40	to Bradford (F. Sq)	11.20
10.35	to Manchester (L. Rd)	13.00

17 July-4 September (8 days operated)

08.16	to Liverpool (L. St)	10.31

31 July-28 August (5 days operated)

08.00	to Sheffield (Mid)	10.23

* The 'Pines Express'

So there was a total of 170 southbound, and 146 northbound regular expresses in the summer of 1954, with relief and extra workings in addition.

By 1960 the number of trains had increasingly declined and 8 September 1962 saw the last of the summer expresses over the Somerset and Dorset. This was the last day of the 'Pines Express' and to fit the occasion it was hauled by Standard '9F' 2-10-0 No 92220 *Evening Star* turned out immaculately by the proud, but sad men of Bath Green Park depot. In this year there had been only ten southbound and eight northbound expresses. The Cleethorpes train had been routed to Exmouth and Sidmouth instead of Bournemouth two years earlier and locomotives changed at Templecombe, the train travelling down the LSWR line via Axminster and Seaton Junction. When the summer Saturday services were withdrawn from the Somerset and Dorset line after the 1962 season, many were routed for the future via Oxford and Reading including the 'Pines'. Further reductions then took place including the withdrawal of the 'Pines Express' which last ran on 4 March 1967, but which was restored in a different form with the 1979/80 timetable. By 1970 there were six northbound and seven southbound Saturdays-only expresses to and from Liverpool, Birmingham, York, Leeds, Sheffield and Bradford, and one overnight train from Leeds to Poole. Most of these trains terminated at Poole, approached down the 1 in 60 gradient of Parkstone bank.

After establishment as a Midland/LSW joint line in 1875, the Somerset and Dorset always had a very interesting and varied collection of locomotives on its metals, particularly on summer Saturdays in later

Above left: Unusual assistance in the shape of LSW 'T9' 4-4-0 No 30120 for a BR '5' 4-6-0 on the 'Pines' leaving Bath Green Park in the late 1950s. *J. K. Sanders*

Above: The Sheffield portion of the 'Pines Express' passes Binegar on 12 July 1954 with MR '2P' No 40509 assisting 'West Country' Pacific No 34044 *Woolacombe*. *H. Gordon Tidey*

Below: S&DJR '7F' 2-8-0 No 53806 drifts down from Masbury Summit with a northbound holiday express in the late 1950s. *D. E. Esau*

years. Alterations to Regional boundaries had an effect. In 1948 Bath, Templecombe and Highbridge depots were numbered in the LMS/LMR '22' series. Two years later depots were taken over by the Southern and joined their '71' group of sheds. In 1958 the depots again changed their control, to be absorbed by the Western and numbered in the '82' series. In less than 20 years, the four depots had been parts of three different Regions. During this post-nationalisation period the locomotive types varied enormously. At first, the old S&DJR and Midland designs predominated, then Standard designs were gradually introduced. Then came a few Southern classes and, later, ex-GWR designs. Certainly on summer Saturdays the combination of locomotives on the holiday expresses was never predictable.

Before 1950 the Saturday traffic was largely in the hands of five Stanier Class '5' 4-6-0s (Nos 44826/830/ 839/945 and 45440) and the LMS and SDJR '4F' 0-6-0s. However, with the increasing number of trains a few of the very new LMS design Class '4' (Nos 43012/013/017/036/047) were transferred to Bath. At this time nearly every one of the summer trains had to be piloted. The Midland '2P' 4-4-0s were

Above: The southbound 'Pines' passes Templecombe mpd — and '7F' 2-8-0 No 53810 — behind rebuilt 'West Country' Pacific No 34047 *Callington* on 1 July 1961. *J. C. Haydon*

Below: New and old S&D motive power. LMS '2P' 4-4-0 No 40569 and BR '9F' 2-10-0 No 92006 combine forces on the northbound 'Pines Express' during September 1961. *G. W. Morrison*

maximum for the 'Black 5s'. Examples of the locomotives used can be seen from six trains noted on 5 August 1950:–see Table 2.

In the summer of 1951 the 'West Country' Pacifics of the Southern first made their appearance. There was great hope that, like the '7F' 2-8-0s, they could haul 10 coaches up the grades unassisted but after unconvincing trials with No 34109 that March, when slipping was the major problem, the limit had to be set at 270 tons, the same as the Stanier Class '5s'. Piloting continued with the excellent, little '2P' 4-4-0s. The Ivatt 2-6-0s returned north in mid-1953 and during that summer most of the work was shared between the Stanier Class '5s' and the 'West Country' Pacifics with occasional turns by '7Fs' and '4Fs'. The '2Ps' and '4Fs' continued to act as pilots and, occasionally, a '3F' 0-6-0 to give it a change from loitering along the Highbridge branch.

In May 1954 three brand-new BR Standard Class '5s' (Nos 73050-52) were delivered to the S&D, replacing three of the 'Black 5s'. Gradually, more Standard '5s' replaced the Stanier '5s' so that by 1957 only No 45440 of the latter remained. This locomotive was one of the original batch sent by the LMS in 1938 and it had been the first Class '5' to haul the 'Pines Express' over the S&D.

so employed on most trains though the '4F' 0-6-0s were used. The eleven S&D '7F' 2-8-0s were tried on the Saturday trains with great success. At first they were only used in an emergency but from 1952 were used on regular Saturday turns. Their advantage lay in their ability to haul 10 coaches, or 315 tons, over Masbury unassisted; this compared with the 270 tons

Table 2		Train engine	Pilot
07.33	ex-Nottingham (Mid)	S&D '7F' 2-8-0 No 53805	LMS '2P' 4-4-0 No 40698
06.52	ex-Cleethorpes	S&D '4F' 0-6-0 No 44557	LMS '4F' 0-6-0 No 44146
07.45	ex-Bradford (F. Sq)	S&D '4F' 0-6-0 No 44559	LMS '4F' 0-6-0 No 44424
10.25	ex-Manchester (L. Rd)	LMS '4F' 0-6-0 No 44422	LMS '2P' 4-4-0 No 569
10.35	ex-Liverpool (L. St)	LMS '4' 2-6-0 No 43013	LMS '4F' 0-6-0 No 44417
/10.40	ex-Manchester (L. Rd)		
09.45*	to Manchester	LMS '5' 4-6-0 No 44945	S&D '2P' 4-4-0 No 40634

* The 'Pines Express'

Table 3
The first S&D summer Saturday workings of 1954 (19 June)

Time	Route	Train engine	Pilot
09.13	ex-Birmingham (N. St)	BR '5' 4-6-0 No 73051	LMS '2P' 4-4-0 No 40697
07.35	ex-Nottingham (Mid)	SR 'WC' 4-6-2 No 34040	LMS '2P' 4-4-0
09.25	to Manchester (L. Rd)/Liverpool (L. St)	SR 'WC' 4-6-2 No 34042	MR '2P' 4-4-0 No 40527
09.45	to Manchester (L. Rd)	SR 'WC' 4-6-2 No 34043	S&D '2P' 4-4-0 No 40634
09.55	to Leeds (City)	BR '5' 4-6-0 No 73050	LMS '2P' 4-4-0 No 40563
10.05	to Cleethorpes	BR '5' 4-6-0 No 73052	LMS '2P' 4-4-0 No 40700

Up to 1960 the pattern remained roughly the same. The Standard Class '4' 4-6-0s, three of which were introduced in 1955 (Nos 75071-73), occasionally worked as either pilot or train engines, the Somerset and Dorset '7Fs' were used more and more and the SR rebuilt 'WC' Pacifics first made their appearance with No 34039 in 1959. Strange pairings occurred from time to time when careful arrangements did not work out as planned. On 2 August 1958, for example, the 10.20 'Pines Express' from Manchester was hauled by 'West Country' class Pacific No 34099 *Lynmouth* with another Pacific, No 34044 *Woolacombe*, as pilot. Another spectacular example occurred on 4 July 1959 when the 07.35 from Nottingham was hauled by '7F' 2-8-0s No 53802 with No 53804 as pilot.

Then, in 1960, a major motive power innovation took place. After successful trials that March, four BR Standard Class '9F' 2-10-0s were introduced

(Nos 92203-206). At last the authorities had found large locomotives that could haul 400 tons unassisted over the Bath-Evercreech Jn section but sadly it was almost too late. In the background plans for diverting the diminishing number of trains were being prepared, and for only three summers these magnificent engines appeared on the S&D hauling twelve coaches unassisted up to Masbury summit. Strangely enough, two of them reappeared in 1963 when no heavy trains were left! At one time the 'Clan' Pacifics allocated to the Scottish Region were considered for transfer to Bath, but instead the Western Region preferred the '9Fs' which were fitted with tablet catchers before going to Bath in June 1960. At this stage, Standard Class '5s' and Bournemouth-allocated Southern

Below: The last days of the 'Pines' over the S&D route. BR '4' 4-6-0 No 75023 assists a '9F' 2-10-0 out of Bath on the southbound train in September 1962. *S. J. Skerman*

Pacifics were usually in charge of other trains. The Cleethorpes train, now travelling to and from Exmouth, had become a regular duty for an unassisted '7F' northbound and a '2P' assisted by a '4F' going south. On 20 August 1960 the northbound train was too heavy for '7F' No 53801 alone and LMS '3F' 0-6-0T No 47275 was attached at Evercreech and proudly headed the train bunker-first as far as Binegar. A month previous, on 2 July, the Cleethorpes train was observed at Bath with '2P' 4-4-0 No 40696 bunker-first having assisted No 53808.

As the need for piloting declined and in view of the age of the locomotives, the '2P' 4-4-0s were gradually withdrawn from 1960. What piloting was still necessary was taken over by Standard Class '4' 4-6-0s, and more were allocated to Bath and Templecombe. The last six '2Ps' were in action during 1961 and the following year only the Standard '4s' were used, apart from an occasional stranger, particularly the GWR Collett '2251' class 0-6-0s, which had recently arrived at Templecombe in place of the Midland '3F' 0-6-0s.

In 1961 a different set of '9Fs' (Nos 92000/001/006/212) was allocated to Bath for the summer, and another four the next year (Nos 92001/210/233/245). That August, No 92210 was fortuitously exchanged for No 92220 *Evening Star* which arrived on the S&D in poor condition. This was soon rectified by Bath depot and on its first Saturday in action, 11 August, it was observed hauling the northbound 'Pines'. Occasionally, 'foreign' '9Fs' were commandeered; for

Below: The 08.40 (SO) Bournemouth-Derby crosses Prestleigh Viaduct behind BR '9F' 2-10-0 No 92245 in the summer of 1962. *G. A. Richardson*

Below right: A last chance for a typical S&D route pairing as '7F' No 53807 and a '4F' 0-6-0 work the 08.15 Bath Green Park-Bournemouth West on 6 June 1964, prior to use on a railtour that day. Seen here at Wincanton. *M. Pope*

example, on three consecutive Saturdays in July 1961, No 92152 of Saltley and Nos 92059/078 of Toton worked overnight turns to Bournemouth, returning with the 09.50 to Leeds. The last '9F' was seen over the S&D on 12 June 1965 when No 92238 headed a Warwickshire Railway Society special.

The last day of summer Saturday workings over the Somerset & Dorset was 8 September 1962. Three '9Fs', two 'West Country' Pacifics, a '7F', and a Standard Class '4' 4-6-0 handled the expresses, with two Standard Class '4s', two Collett 0-6-0s and a Standard Class '5' as the pilots. It will be noted that the majority of the locomotives were of BR Standard design. The Southern were well represented, the Western, too, and even one of the indefatigable S&D '7F' 2-8-0s was game to the last, but there was a complete absence of a Midland or LMS-design locomotive on that Saturday's expresses. A full circle had turned. In 1948, the holiday special locomotives were almost entirely Midland, but fifteen years later, none.

Not until the final weekend before the closure of the Somerset and Dorset three and a half years later was there the real sight of a double-headed express again. On Sunday, 6 March 1966, the very last train over the line was hauled by Southern Pacifics, Nos 34013 *Okehampton* (a rebuild) and unrebuilt No 34057 *Biggin Hill*. Together they probably made the fastest climb ever up to Masbury. After the pilotman had been put down at Midsomer Norton and the train had crossed over from the wrong line, it was driven flat out to Masbury Summit. The train passed Binegar at an estimated 60mile/h, but one of the engines was eased slightly at the summit. It was certainly a spectacle and a grand finale as the two Pacifics disappeared into the night at the head of their nine-coach special, leaving behind them a trail of fire beside the line. It was both the death of the S&D as a railway and the last memory of those postwar busy summer Saturdays.

Table 4
An average summer Saturday on the S&D — 12 August 1961
SOUTHBOUND

		Bath (arr)	Bournemouth W. (arr)	Train engine	Pilot engine
22.00 (FO)	ex-Sheffield (Mid)	02.35	05.00	'9F' 92001	
20.25 (FO)	ex-Bradford (F. Sq)	03.15	06.01	'9F' 92006	
22.28 (FO)	ex-Manchester (L. Rd)	04.10	06.44	'9F' 92000	
09.05	ex-Bristol	09.53	12.54	BR '5' 73047	'2P' 40697
07.42	ex-Birmingham (N. St)	10.30	13.17	BR '5' 73051	
09.08	ex-Birmingham (N. St)	11.55	14.55	BR '5' 73052	'2P' 40700
07.35	ex-Nottingham (Mid)	12.20	15.07	'7F' 53807	
07.00	ex-Cleethorpes	14.10 — to Exmouth		'4F' 44422	'2P' 40569
09.35	ex-Sheffield (Mid)	14.30	17.20	'9F' 92001	
07.43	ex-Bradford (F. Sq)	14.50	17.35	'9F' 92006	
10.25*	ex-Manchester (L. Rd)	15.30	18.08	'WC' 34045	'2P' 40564
10.20	ex-Liverpool	16.20	19.05	'WC' 34041	BR '4' 75027
10.55	ex-Manchester (L. Rd)				

NORTHBOUND

Bournemouth (dep)		Bath (arr)	Train engine	Pilot engine
08.40	to Bradford (F. Sq)	11.14	'9F' 92001	
09.25	to Liverpool (L. St)/Manchester (L. Rd)	11.45	'WC' 34045	'2P' 40569
09.45*	to Manchester (L. Rd)	11.56	'9F' 92006	'2P' 40634
09.55	to Leeds (City)	12.25	'9F' 92000	
10.05	to Derby (Mid)	12.45	BR '5' 73054	BR '4' 75027
10.32	to Manchester (L. Rd)	13.00	'WC' 34043	'2P' 40697
11.12	to Sheffield (Mid)	13.49	'7F' 53810	'2P' 40564
10.40†	to Cleethorpes	14.10	'7F' 53806	3210
12.00‡		14.35	BR '5' 73050	GWR
12.20	to Nottingham (Mid)	14.54	'WC' 34041	'2P' 40700
15.40	to Bristol	18.56	BR '5' 73047	
19.25	to Bristol	21.53	BR '5' 73051	

* The 'Pines Express'
† From Exmouth
‡ Relief

Inter-City commuting

P. A. TURVEY

All photographs by Brian Morrison

For quite a number of days during the first six months of 1978 I travelled by Inter-City services between Plymouth and Exeter. In fact, the journeys began in October 1977 but it was not until the following January that I realised that details of the journeys might be worth recording. So, I take the liberty of commenting on the services used from memory rather than from records, because certain journeys, including one failure on Rattery bank, were undertaken before I began keeping exact details.

The journey from Plymouth to Exeter by rail is very interesting, exactly fifty-two miles, some eight miles longer than the more direct route provided by the A38

road, now dual-carriageway. In fact, it takes me about fifty minutes for a one-way journey from my home to the centre of Exeter by car, but at least thirty minutes longer if I travel by train. The railway takes a fairly roundabout route seeking the easiest grades and following river valleys and the coastline.

The track runs down-grade from Plymouth North Road station past Laira traction depot and beside the river Plym before the start of the first of the famous South Devon banks. At 1 in 42, Hemerdon presents quite an obstacle and most trains lose speed considerably before breasting the summit at about 300ft above sea-level. On one or two occasions the train came to a halt, but there was never a failure requiring assistance from another train or locomotive. On one journey, passengers were entertained to the sight of a

Left: Class 50 No 50.005 *Collingwood* on Dainton bank with the 13.30 Paddington-Penzance of 2 July 1979.

Above: Alongside the beaches between Dawlish and Teignmouth comes No 50.012 *Benbow* with the 10.30 Paddington-Plymouth on 6 July 1979.

small, chubby guard dashing through the train muttering, 'he's going to stop, he's going to stop . . .'.

During the twelve months of my journeys Hermerdon had the added interest of the gas board laying a main supply pipe across the main line. This was completed by tunnelling under the railway but without any apparent disruption. From Hemerdon summit the line winds almost contouring around the southern edges of Dartmoor. The journey is smooth as the train hastens over viaducts, through cuttings and overbridges with the heights of Dartmoor to one side and the valleys of the several south-flowing rivers on the other. After passing through Marley Tunnel there is the slow, serpentine run down Rattery bank to the tidal limit of the river Dart at Totnes. Trains stopping there slow even more to take the turnout from the main line to slide gently into Totnes' austere platform. Passengers on passing trains usually experience a sudden surge as the locomotive is notched up and the driver puts on power to climb the western approaches

to Dainton. Railway enthusiasts on the train are able to gather a glimpse of the past as Totnes Riverside on the Dart Valley Railway passes by and at the right time of the year can glimpse the smoke and steam of trains plying to and from Buckfastleigh. The two railways obviously enjoy meeting for there is usually an encouraging and welcoming toot on the steam locomotive whistles and an equally enthusiastic response from the two-tone hooters of the passing diesel. Then comes the main line's climb up to Dainton summit.

The passage through Dainton Tunnel is usually fairly slow followed by a restrained meander past Stoneycombe quarry down to Aller Junction and the approaches to Newton Abbot. Here, trains have returned almost to sea-level and are about to run beside the beautiful beaches of Teignmouth and Dawlish. In rough weather, and at high tide, the waves burst against the retaining wall and envelope passing trains in spray. In my year of travelling I was lucky as no real damage was done to the track and my journeys were not interrupted. From Dawlish Warren there is a smooth, curving, level run beside the estuary of the river Exe past Exminster and into Exeter St Davids.

On my trips I liked to enjoy the views between Exeter and Newton Abbot and usually travelled for

that part of the journey in whatever form of catering vehicle was included in the train so that I could gaze at the passing seascape over a cup of hot coffee. Generally, Paddington-West of England trains have a restaurant car with buffet facilities and trains on the south-west/north-east route have a buffet car only. On every journey the crews provided a good service in an acceptable environment. Most appreciated were those who brought coffee through the train, a new

Above: Inter-City 125 workings were foreshadowed on 2 July 1979 as No 50.028 *Tiger* took the 10.30 Paddington-Plymouth past IC125 set No 253.017 on a crew training run at Newton Abbot.

Below: Newton Abbot on 2 July 1979 with Class 47/4 No 47.531 bringing the 13.48 Plymouth-Paddington into the station.

experience to travellers in the south-west which appeared to come with the introduction of the air-conditioned Mk2E/F coaches.

Although I have been interested in railways for nearly all my life, I have never been a devotee of logging rail journeys. In fact, I have travelled by train on only a few occasions since I gained a driving licence many years ago. A year's commuting between Plymouth and Exeter was something special for I have never been able to make so many rail journeys before and do not expect to have the opportunity again.

All that I did was to record starting times and arrival times, classes of locomotive and anything of special interest. The two charts show details of journeys in each direction. Timekeeping was reckoned by a departure or arrival within sixty seconds of the particular minute concerned. Not surprisingly, the journeys from Plymouth to Exeter were the most punctual and nearly all the unpunctual runs were only a minute or so out, although there were one or two exceptions, usually on the 08.40 ex-Plymouth which had met with delays in Cornwall before it arrived in Plymouth. On some journeys difficulties were experienced when adding the catering vehicles to the Penzance portion at Plymouth.

Timekeeping was much less satisfactory with trains departing from Exeter, particularly with cross-country expresses from the north. Most notorious was the

15.11 departure, the 10.23 ex-Manchester. Before I started keeping records, this train failed to arrive more than once. One day it arrived an hour late and then the locomotive failed on Rattery to add insult to injury. During the recording period the Manchester train's performance was apparently reasonable, largely because I made every effort not to use it! Trains from Paddington usually ran with immaculate regularity, because there seemed to be ample recovery time available and trains frequently arrived in Exeter with more than ten minutes to spare before departure. Most interesting is the fact that most of these trains arrived in Plymouth early and the punctual arrivals recorded usually indicate an early arrival; in my experience, anything up to thirteen minutes was cut off the journey. This wasn't a bad effort if you take into consideration that the 16.06 from Exeter was booked to take 64 minutes for the tortuous fifty-two miles, but I recorded one trip to take no more than 51 minutes, at an average speed of over 60mile/h start-to-stop, which is pretty good considering the various permanent speed reductions on some curved sections en route, at Newton Abbot and at Totnes. I remembered this journey well because it was obvious that the driver was using the full power of the Class 50 diesel-electric, No 50.049. The climb up to Dainton was quite thrilling with the exhaust roaring and with speed being maintained to the top. Most trains dropped to what

Above: Class 47 No 47.482's train is Paddington-bound as it drops down the incline out of Dainton Tunnel.

Below: Class 45/0 No 45.031 approaches Totnes on 1 July 1979 at the head of the 09.25 Manchester Piccadilly-Plymouth.

seemed like little more than a walking speed in the tunnel. But No 50.049 surged on, up Rattery as though the 1 in 46-90 gradients weren't there and wound itself through the curves at South Brent and Ivybridge in a most exhilarating manner. It made me think that with the Class 50 locomotives and determined driving the Plymouth-Exeter services could make the railway very competitive compared with the sort of times that car drivers can make along the parallel A38 dual-carriageway.

In all, it was an interesting year of commuter travell-

Above: Class 50 No 50.036 *Victorious* nears Totnes station with the 15.01 Penzance-Paddington on 4 July 1979.

Below: Class 47/0 No 47.072 winds out of Totnes with a down schools excursion on 4 July 1979.

Below right: Class 50 No 50.001 *Dreadnought* accelerates out of Newton Abbot with the 08.34 Penzance-Paddington on 2 July 1979.

ing over a stretch of British Rail then remote from the IC125 high-speed timings of the London to Bristol and South Wales services and the speed exploits of the West and East Coast routes to Scotland. There was some evidence of slowing down with the 1978/9 timetable. This was to give some allowance for the engineer-ing work being undertaken 'up the line' in preparation for the IC125 services from Paddington to the West of England which came in from October 1979. I look forward to comparing my runs on locomotive-hauled trains in 1978 with IC125s running between the two south-western cities.

Table 1
Up trains — Plymouth-Exeter Jan-June 1978

Departure Plymouth*	Arrival Exeter*	Booked Times*	Stopping at	No of journeys	Punctual Dep	Late Dep	Punctual Arr	Late Arr	Usual loco	Other locos used	Notes
08.13 (08.15)	09.20 (09.26)	67 (69)	Totnes Newton Abbot	13	12	1	12	1	Class 47	Class 46/45	
08.40 (08.38)	09.38 (09.40)	58 (62)	—	26	17	9	14	12	Class 50	Class 47/4	A B C
10.50	11.48 (11.52)	58 (62)	—	1	1	—	1	—	Class 50	—	
12.39 (12.40)	13.39 (13.45)	60 (65)	—	5	4	1	3	2	Class 46	Class 47/45	D E
Total:				45	34	11	30	15			

Notes:
A. Journey apparently delayed by light engine proceeding to Totnes
B. Locomotive and additional coaches could not couple with Penzance portion at Plymouth causing one late departure
C. One 08.40 departure not recorded — train did not arrive from Penzance
D. One late arrival in Exeter owing to delays at Newton Abbot
E. Delayed owing to derailment at Newton Abbot which caused single-track working
* Summer 1978/9 timetable times in brackets

Down trains — Exeter-Plymouth Jan-June 1978

Departure Exeter*	Arrival Plymouth*	Booked Times*	Stopping at	No of journeys	Punctual Dep	Late Dep	Punctual Arr	Late Arr	Usual loco	Other loco used	Notes
11.13	12.20	67	Newton Abbot	3	1	2	2	1	Class 50	—	—
12.10	13.19	69	Totnes	1	1	—	—	1	Class 50	—	—
13.05 (13.07)	14.11 (14.13)	66 (66)	—	8	4	4	7	1	Class 45	Class 46	A B
13.27	14.40	73	Newton Abbot	2	—	2	2	2	—	Class 50 Class 47/4	C D
14.00	15.04 'Cornish Riviera'	64	—	3	1	2	1	2	Class 50	—	E
15.11 (15.12)	16.25 (16.28)	74 (76)	Newton Abbot Totnes	8	6	2	6	2	Class 45	—	F G
16.06 (16.04)	17.10 (17.09)	64 (65)	—	12	8	4	11	1	Class 50	—	H
17.02	18.16	74	Newton Abbot Totnes	1	—	1	1	—	dmu from Barnstaple		
Total				38	21	17	28	10			

Notes:
A. 1.6.78. 45.009 failed in St Davids. 47.033 took over and was 25 minutes late all the way
B. 31.5.78. This train was announced running $1\frac{1}{2}$ hours late
C. 50.029 arrived 15.05 in Plymouth
D. 47.499 made additional stops owing to failure of preceding train (31.5.78)
E. This journey recorded from Paddington — preceding Paignton train failed at Somerton with loco 47.508. 50.039 propelled both trains including 19 coaches to Taunton reaching a maximum speed of 65mile/h. At Taunton 47.090 left empty china clay wagons on main line and hauled failure to Exeter. There 47.504 took over. 50.039 arrived Paignton at 15.42 — 38 minutes late.
F. 45.003 on 15.12 departed 15.40
G. Actually caught train at Newton Abbot on one occasion running 29 minutes late
H. This train usually arrived early — 30.1.78. 50.049 arrived Plymouth 13mins early completing the run in 51 minutes
* Summer 1978/9 timetable times in brackets

Class 25 Bo-Bo diesel electrics at Kettering in December 1979.   *R. Payne*